Contents for guide

Foreword	v
Acknowledgements	vi
Introduction	vii
Setting the context	vii
Contents of Children Act 2004	1
The Children Act 2004	4
References	105
Further reading	107
List of Acts	110
List of acronyms	111

For each and every child

Foreword

One of the recurrent problems in offering integrated services to children has been in establishing a common understanding between all the professional groups involved with children. Similarly, I am only too aware of the difficulty for lay people in understanding legislation that is both very complex and inaccessible to the normal reader.

So, I am very pleased to introduce this plain guide to the Children Act 2004, which has succeeded in bringing together, in one place, the context that led to the Children Act, the legislation itself and a parallel commentary on the legislation – in plain language.

It is obviously the letter of the law that is tested in court and the interpretation in this volume makes no claim to pre-judge the court's interpretation of every detail of the Children Act. However, as a plain guide for the wide range of professionals and others working to secure the very best for all of our children, I am confident that it will help to promote a wide understanding of the spirit of the legislation.

Baroness Helena Kennedy, QC

Acknowledgements

Officials from the Department for Education and Skills have worked very closely with a wide range of partners in the statutory and voluntary sector to ensure that this legislation, and the forthcoming guidance, will assist in delivering our ambitions for children's services and we are grateful for their comments and clarifications as the legislation has developed.

We are also grateful to the scrutiny work of MPs and Peers on the Bill during its passage through Parliament. Ministerial replies to questions have improved our understanding of the legislation and, we hope, the text of this plain guide.

We have received support and advice from members of the Inter-Agency Group and other individuals involved in delivering the new agenda for children. We hope that the usefulness of this book will, in some small way, repay them for their help.

We are indebted to the staff of the National Foundation for Educational Research for their success in getting this book to market so soon after the *Children Act 2004* received Royal Assent. In particular we wish to thank the Communications, Marketing and Information Services department for their encouragement and perseverance. We would also like to thank our external reviewers, in particular Beatrice Cooper for her proofreading, technical knowledge and overall support for this project.

Responsibility for the comments and judgements in this book remains with us. The book does not purport to give legal guidance or to offer an authoritative interpretation of the law.

Chris Waterman
John Fowler

Introduction

This *plain guide to the Children Act 2004* establishes a 'one stop shop' for professionals and others with an interest in the developing children's agenda.

The heart of this plain guide is the Act itself, which is reproduced, but with a parallel explanation in plain language. This introduction contains background information on how the legislation came about, and a further reading section provides further information on source material. A forward look at dates for the commencement of the Act's requirements and the publication of DfES guidance can be found at the end of this introduction.

Setting the context

Victoria Climbie

Victoria Climbie was sent to Europe by her parents to be looked after and educated by her great-aunt, Marie-Therese Kouao in November 1998. Victoria died, aged eight, on 25 February 2000. Her carers, her great-aunt and her partner Carl Manning, were convicted of her murder on 12 January 2001.

While in the care of her great-aunt, Victoria came into contact with four social services departments, three housing departments, two specialist child protection teams of the Metropolitan Police, two hospitals and a family centre managed by the NSPCC. No-one noted or did anything about the fact that she was not in school or had continuing general practitioner care.

As with many previous cases, the statutory services had failed in their duty to protect a vulnerable child from being murdered by carers.

The Report of the Victoria Climbie Inquiry

As a result of the information that came to light in the investigation into the circumstances of Victoria's death, the Government established on 20 April 2001 three statutory inquiries, collectively known as the Victoria Climbie Inquiry, chaired by Lord Laming, a former Director of Social Services and Social Services Chief Inspector.

The *Report of the Victoria Climbie Inquiry* (Cm. 5730) (UK.Parliament.HoC, 2003) was published on 28 January 2003. Lord Laming's view was that, although there were shortcomings among 'the often hapless front line staff'

> *The greatest failure rests with the senior managers and members of the organisations concerned whose responsibility it was to ensure that the services they provided to children such as Victoria were properly financed, staffed and able to deliver good quality services to children and families. They must be accountable.*
>
> (The Victoria Climbie Inquiry, 2003)

The report outlined three areas in the recommendations:

1   a fundamental change in the mind-set of managers in key public services, who must see their role in terms of the quality of services delivered at the front door rather than in administrating bureaucratic and sometimes self-serving procedures

2   a clear and unambiguous line of managerial accountability both within and across public services

3   the current arrangements of Area Child Protection Committees or any proposal for a national child protection agency, should be replaced by a new National Agency for children and families. This Agency should have powers to ensure that all of the key services affecting children and families – health, housing and police – carry out their duties in an efficient and effective way. The Chief Executive of this agency could undertake the functions of a Children's Commissioner for England. The Agency should report to a new ministerial committee for children, chaired by a minister of cabinet rank who would be responsible for ensuring that policies, legislation and departmental initiatives affecting children and families are properly considered, financed and coordinated. Similar arrangements need to operate at a local level.

The Inter-Agency Group

In February 2002, the President of the Association of Directors of Social Services wrote to a number of key professional and voluntary organisations suggesting a meeting to share some of the issues that were being put to the Victoria Climbie Inquiry.

From this first meeting, the Inter-Agency Group was formed, comprising representatives of the

- Association of Chief Education Officers, now known as the Association of Directors of Education and Children's Services

- Association of Directors of Social Services

- Barnardo's

- the Children's Society

- the Confederation of Education Service Managers now known as the Confederation of Education and Children's Services Managers

- the Connaught Group

- the Local Government Association

- the Metropolitan Police

- the National Children's Bureau
- National Children's Homes
- National Council for Voluntary Childcare Organisations
- NHS Confederation
- National Society for the Prevention of Cruelty to Children
- Society of Local Authority Chief Executives.

This group has met regularly since February 2002 and has offered a very powerful voice to Government on the issues arising from the Inquiry. The IAG was a key means of establishing a common understanding between the statutory and voluntary sectors of their respective responsibilities and the measures needed to improve services for vulnerable children.

The group was in frequent contact with ministers and senior civil servants across Government and was used as a sounding board for proposed policy developments (for example in the drafting of the Green Paper, *Every Child Matters* (HM Treasury, 2003)).

It continues to meet regularly with the Children's Minister and DfES officials.

The Minister for Children

After very considerable discussion and debate within Government, the Prime Minister announced, on 17 June 2003, the creation of a new post based in the DfES – a children's minister, officially 'the Minister of State for Children, Young People and Families' to provide integrated leadership and responsibility for children's services and family policy across Whitehall. The post has responsibility for children's social care, childcare and pre-school support, careers advice and family support and legal services. Staff have moved from other departments to form a new DfES directorate, the Children, Young People and Families Directorate.

The first task of the new minister, Margaret Hodge MP, previously minister for higher education, was to oversee the publication of the Green Paper *Every Child Matters* (HM Treasury, 2003).

Every Child Matters

Initially, it was hoped that the Green Paper would be published in the summer of 2003, but with the appointment of the Children's Minister and the changes in departmental responsibilities that accompanied the appointment, the Green Paper *Every Child Matters* (Cm 5860) (HM Treasury, 2003) was presented to Parliament by Charles Clarke, Secretary of State for Education and Skills, on 8 September 2003 along with the

Government's response to the Climbie Inquiry *Keeping Children Safe* (Cm 5861) (DfES, DoH and HO, 2003).

The foreword was written by the Prime Minister and the introduction by Paul Boateng MP, who had led the development of the Green Paper while he was Minister for Young People at the Home Office and prior to his promotion to Chief Secretary of the Treasury.

The Government's aim, as set out in the Green Paper, is to ensure that every child has the chance to fulfil his/her potential by reducing levels of education failure, ill health, substance misuse, teenage pregnancy, abuse and neglect, crime and anti-social behaviour among children and young people. New structures would be provided to help the education, health and welfare services to work together better and to help coordinate their work with the other public and voluntary services working with children.

The Green Paper also introduced the 'five outcomes' for children's services following consultation with children, young people and families. They are to:

- be healthy
- stay safe
- enjoy and achieve
- make a positive contribution
- achieve economic well-being.

The translation of these outcomes to legal language can be found in the Act in s. 10(2) for England and s. 25(2) for Wales as the areas for improving the well-being of children:

- physical and mental health and emotional well-being
- protection from harm and neglect
- education, training and recreation
- the contribution made by them (children and young people) to society
- social and economic well-being.

The Children's Commissioner also has to be concerned with the outcomes under s. 2(3).

Children Bill and Every Child Matters – Next Steps

The *Children Bill* and *Every Child Matters – Next Steps* (DfES, 2004c) were published on 3 March 2004. *Next Steps* summarises the comments on the Green Paper and gives an overview of the legislative changes proposed in the Bill. There are further chapters on the Government's vision for children's services and working in partnership.

The Children Bill was introduced into the House of Lords and completed its Lords stages before the Summer recess on 19 July 2004. The Commons Stages took place in the Autumn with Royal Assent on 15 November 2004.

Every Child Matters: Change for Children

On 1 December 2004, *Every Child Matters: Change for Children* (DfES, 2004b) was launched under the signature of 16 ministers from 13 government departments. It sets out the national framework for the local change programme needed to deliver integrated services. The document sets out the Government's timetable for introducing the Act and the publication dates of the statutory guidance. Information on the implementation and guidance timetables is reproduced at the end of this introduction. Draft guidance covering aspects of s. 12, 18 and 19 is referred to in the notes on each section.

Other recent developments

Although this book focuses on the *Children Act 2004*, implementing the Act is only part of the Government's overall *Every Child Matters* strategy.

Bichard Inquiry

Sir Michael Bichard was asked by the Home Secretary to lead an independent inquiry into child protection measures, record keeping, vetting and information sharing in Humberside Police and Cambridgeshire Constabulary, following Ian Huntley's conviction in December 2003 for the murders of Jessica Chapman and Holly Wells. The report of the inquiry was published on 14 June 2004 (as HC 653) and the recommendations in the report will have implications for the establishment of information sharing procedures in the Act.

National Service Framework for Children, Young People and Maternity Services

The *National Service Framework for Children, Young People and Maternity Services* (DOH, 2004) was published jointly by the Department of Health and DfES on 4 October 2004. The *National Service Framework* provides a 10-year strategy for the NHS to achieve a long-term improvement in children's health by setting standards for children's health and social care. The NSF standards will help the NHS achieve the 'five outcomes' for children's services in the Change for Children programme. The standards will also feed into the new integrated inspection framework.

Choosing health: making health choices easier

The public health White Paper *Choosing health: making health choices easier* (Cm 6374) (UK.Parliament.HOC, 2004) was published on 16 November 2004. The White Paper shows how the Primary Care Trusts can be fully involved in the new Children and Young People's Plans; this includes tackling health inequalities among children and young people in order to break the cycle of deprivation. The integration of health services through the Children's Trust model, and the development of children's centres and extended schools are promoted as important elements of improving the health of children.

Wales

The Act makes separate provision in Wales for children's services, recognising the different paths travelled by the London and Cardiff administrations since devolution in 1999. While the duty to cooperate to improve well-being, planning, duty to safeguard and promote welfare, information databases and Local Safeguarding Children Boards are largely the same, this is not the case with local leadership. Wales retains both a Chief Education Officer and Director of Social Services posts, preferring to require Children's Services Authorities to appoint a lead director for children and young people. There is no equivalent provision to Joint Area Reviews and the Welsh Assembly Government has announced that there is no expectation that the duty to cooperate will lead to Children's Trusts. Wales has had a Children's Commissioner since 2001.

The Assembly's strategy was set out in *Children and Young People: A Framework for Partnership* (Welsh Assembly Government, 2000) and updated in *Children and Young People: Rights to Action* (Welsh Assembly Government, 2004).

Implementing the Act: the issues

While this book is about explaining the Act, the authors offer this short introduction to some of the issues that those responsible for children's services will have to tackle if they are to achieve the Act's ambition of getting more effective services for children.

Without doubt, the major challenge is delivering properly integrated services and this requires a cultural change within and between the many professional groups involved with children. Lord Laming has said this requires a 'fundamental change in the mind-set of managers'.

National government

Within central government, the need to join up Whitehall must continue through joint planning between ministers and senior officials in the DfES, DOH and Home Office to meet the needs of children and their families. The test will be in the quality of guidance produced by the Government and the extent that all government policies support the well-being of children.

Within the DfES, there is a continuing need to integrate the policy and planning work of the two new directorates principally involved (the Schools Directorate and the Children, Young People and Families Directorate) so that mutually compatible policies are pursued. The requirement for children's services authorities to produce a Children and Young People's Plan rather than a Single Education Plan is one manifestation of this effort so far.

Local government

Within local government, the requirement to appoint a Director of Children's Services (DCS) and a lead member for children's services has been widely welcomed, and a number of DCSs are already in post. The challenge is to retain experienced managers and build the morale of staff while integrating services and establishing Children's Trusts. This will be an important test of local leadership and offers an unrivalled opportunity for local government to prove its community leadership abilities for all children and their families.

National Health Service

Within the National Health Service, strategic health authorities and primary care trusts, have new responsibilities to cooperate and facilitate joint working. This provides an unrivalled opportunity to reorder and reorganise health services in conjunction with education and social care services around the needs of the child and deliver integrated services to children and families.

Local child protection coordination

Placing the new Local Safeguarding Children Boards on a statutory footing, and placing a duty on local partners to cooperate and coordinate, will give local bodies a local accountability mechanism to ensure the effectiveness of services to safeguard children.

Frontline services

At the frontline, although schools, general practitioners and social landlords are not given an explicit duty on the face of the Act to cooperate (except as bodies that must be involved in the supply of information for the new information sharing arrangements), these services will be critical to the success of the new agenda.

School governors, headteachers, school staff, police, health centre staff and community health services will all have a part to play in achieving the integration of services for children. With the support from the respective authorities and trusts, this can happen and the Act's visionary 'five outcomes', desired by young people as they grow up to adulthood, can become a reality.

Commentary on the Children Act: explanations

Various conventions have been adopted in the comments on the *Children Act 2004* to refer to provisions.

Subsections of sections are always bracketed. For example subsection (2) of section 10 contain the outcomes for children's services and is referred to as section 10(2), or for convenience s. 10(2).

The abbreviation 'ss.' is used when referring to more than one section, for example ss. 31 to 34 are on the Local Safeguarding Children Boards in Wales.

The term 'paragraph' refers to a part of a subsection, for example paragraph (b) of subsection (6) of section 12, or s. 12(6)(b) for short, is the legislative authority for specifying those bodies that must contribute data to the new information sharing arrangements. The term paragraph is also used with Schedules. Thus paragraph 3(2) of Schedule 1, or Schedule 1(3)(2) for short, requires the Secretary of State to involve children in the appointment of the Commissioner.

The term 'Secretary of State'

Care needs to be taken with the term 'Secretary of State'. Powers vested in government ministers are usually given to the 'Secretary of State'. In this Act, the 'Secretary of State' will be the Secretary of State for Education and Skills in many cases, for example, in s. 4 where the Secretary of State has the power to direct the Children's Commissioner to hold an inquiry. Other cases are more complicated. For example, the Secretary of State who issues the statutory guidance under s. 16(2) to Local Safeguarding Children Boards will cover the remit of three Secretary of States, namely Education and Skills, Health and the Home Office. However, the British constitutional principle of Cabinet collective responsibility does not require legislation to specify which Secretary of State, as whichever Secretary of State issues the guidance binds the other Secretaries of State. However in Wales, in the equivalent provision in s. 34(2) and (3), where the education and health functions are devolved to the Assembly, the Secretary of State is still required to consent to the guidance because youth justice has not been devolved. Whether the Secretary of State role is performed by the Secretary of State for Wales or the Home Secretary does not matter because of Cabinet collective responsibility.

Continuing the debate

The authors would be pleased to receive comment on this plain guide. Please email comments to John Fowler at john_fowler@btinternet.com.

Timeline of when statutory requirements come into effect

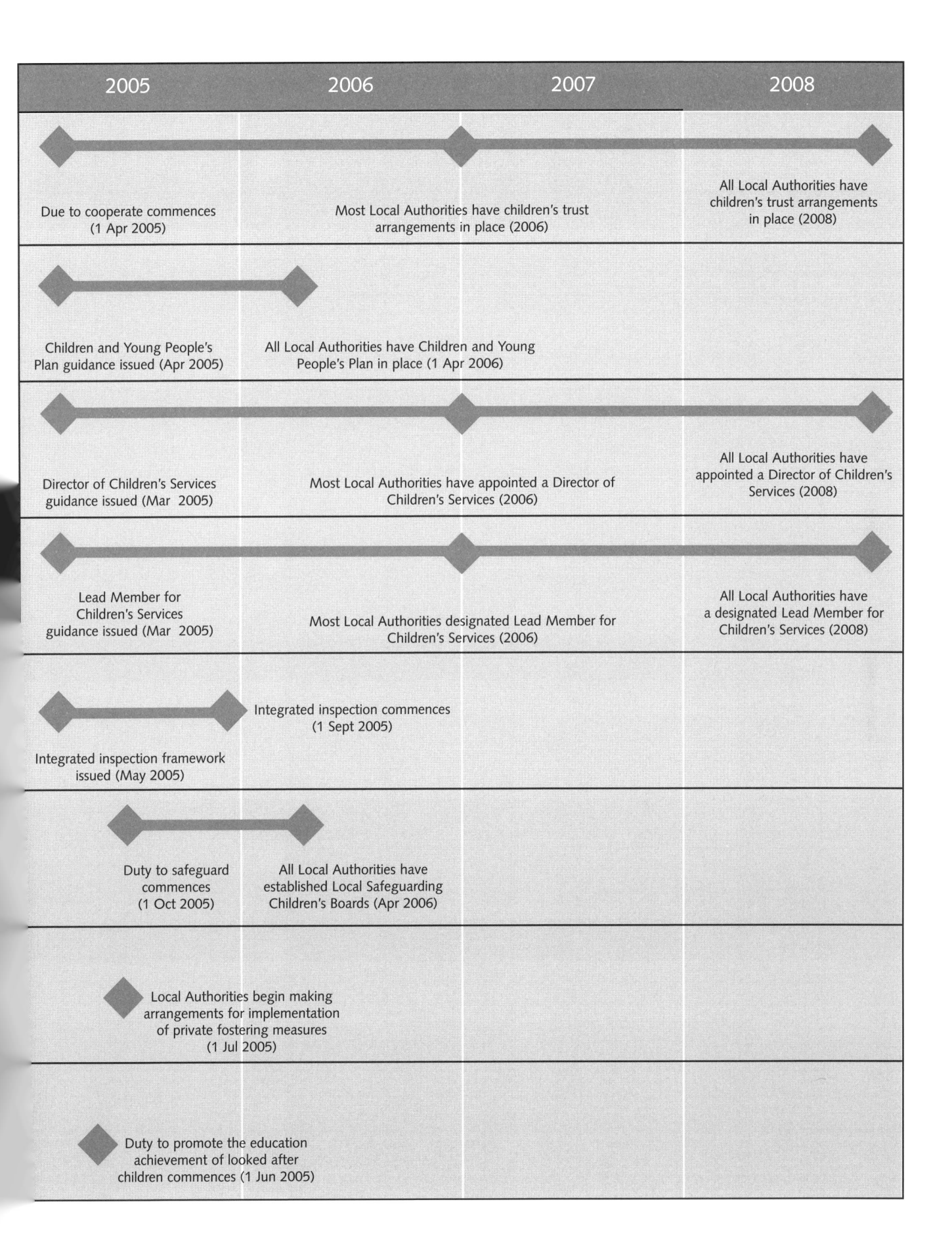

2005	2006	2007	2008
Due to cooperate commences (1 Apr 2005)	Most Local Authorities have children's trust arrangements in place (2006)		All Local Authorities have children's trust arrangements in place (2008)
Children and Young People's Plan guidance issued (Apr 2005)	All Local Authorities have Children and Young People's Plan in place (1 Apr 2006)		
Director of Children's Services guidance issued (Mar 2005)	Most Local Authorities have appointed a Director of Children's Services (2006)		All Local Authorities have appointed a Director of Children's Services (2008)
Lead Member for Children's Services guidance issued (Mar 2005)	Most Local Authorities designated Lead Member for Children's Services (2006)		All Local Authorities have a designated Lead Member for Children's Services (2008)
Integrated inspection framework issued (May 2005) — Integrated inspection commences (1 Sept 2005)			
Duty to safeguard commences (1 Oct 2005)	All Local Authorities have established Local Safeguarding Children's Boards (Apr 2006)		
Local Authorities begin making arrangements for implementation of private fostering measures (1 Jul 2005)			
Duty to promote the education achievement of looked after children commences (1 Jun 2005)			

plain guide to the Children Act 2004

Forward look at publication dates for key documents and guidance consultations

	Nov 2004	Dec 2004	Jan 2005	Feb 2005	Mar 2005	Apr 2005	thereafter
Developing the vision							
Change for Children		published					
Strategy for early years and childcare		published					
CFC Social Care, CJS and Health docs		published					
Green Paper on youth			published				
CFC Schools doc			published				
Local Partnerships							
Director of Children's Services & Lead Member guidance consultation	launch				published		
Working with voluntary and community organisations to deliver change for children		published					
Framework for Inspection of Children's Services consultation		launch					published
Duty to co-operate guidance consultation		launch			published		
Children & Young People's Plan guidance			launch			published	
Safeguarding							
Duty to safeguard & promote welfare guidance consultation		launch					published
Consultation on new regulations, revised Children Act guidance & National Minimum Standards on private fostering		launch					published
LSCB guidance published							published
Parents and Carers							
Response to consultation on Parental Separation Green Paper		issued					
Educational achievement of looked after children guidance consultation			launch				published
Children's Workforce							
Common Core prospectus			published				
Pay and Workforce Strategy			published				
Common Assessment Framework					published		
Multi-agency working and lead professional guidance						published	
Cross-government information sharing guidance							published
ISA guidance							published

xvi

plain guide to the Children Act 2004

Contents of Children Act 2004

Part 1 Children's Commissioner

1 Establishment
2 General function
3 Inquiries initiated by Commissioner
4 Other inquiries held by Commissioner
5 Functions of Commissioner in Wales
6 Functions of Commissioner in Scotland
7 Functions of Commissioner in Northern Ireland
8 Annual reports
9 Care leavers and young persons with learning disabilities

Part 2 Children's services in England

General
10 Co-operation to improve well-being
11 Arrangements to safeguard and promote welfare
12 Information databases

Local Safeguarding Children Boards
13 Establishment of LSCBs
14 Functions and procedure of LSCBs
15 Funding of LSCBs
16 LSCBs: supplementary

Local authority administration
17 Children and young people's plans
18 Director of children's services
19 Lead member for children's services

Inspections of children's services
20 Joint area reviews
21 Framework
22 Co-operation and delegation
23 Sections 20 to 22: interpretation
24 Performance rating of social services

Part 3 Children's services in Wales

General
25 Co-operation to improve well-being: Wales
26 Children and young people's plans: Wales
27 Responsibility for functions under sections 25 and 26

28 Arrangements to safeguard and promote welfare: Wales
29 Information databases: Wales
30 Inspection of functions under this Part

Local Safeguarding Children Boards

31 Establishment of LSCBs in Wales
32 Functions and procedure of LSCBs in Wales
33 Funding of LSCBs in Wales
34 LSCBs in Wales: supplementary

Part 4 Advisory and support services for family proceedings

CAFCASS functions in Wales

35 Functions of the Assembly relating to family proceedings
36 Ancillary powers of the Assembly
37 Welsh family proceedings officers
38 Inspections
39 Protection of children
40 Advisory and support services for family proceedings: supplementary
41 Sharing of information

Transfers

42 Transfer of property from CAFCASS to Assembly
43 Transfer of staff from CAFCASS to Assembly

Part 5 Miscellaneous

Private fostering

44 Amendments to notification scheme
45 Power to establish registration scheme in England
46 Power to establish registration scheme in Wales
47 Expiry of powers in sections 45 and 46

Child minding and day care

48 Child minding and day care

Local authority services

49 Payments to foster parents
50 Intervention
51 Inspection of local education authorities
52 Duty of local authorities to promote educational achievement
53 Ascertaining children's wishes
54 Information about individual children
55 Social services committees
56 Social services functions

Other provisions

57 Fees payable to adoption review panel members
58 Reasonable punishment
59 Power to give financial assistance
60 Child safety orders
61 Children's Commissioner for Wales: powers of entry
62 Publication of material relating to legal proceedings
63 Disclosure of information by Inland Revenue

Part 6 General

64 Repeals
65 Interpretation
66 Regulations and orders
67 Commencement
68 Extent
70 Short title

Schedule 1 – Children's Commissioner
Schedule 2 – Director of children's services: consequential amendments
Schedule 3 – Advisory and support services for family proceedings
Schedule 4 – Child minding and day care
Schedule 5 – Repeals
    Part 1 – Plans
    Part 2 – Child minding and day care
    Part 3 – Inspection of local education authorities
    Part 4 – Social services committees and departments
    Part 5 – Reasonable punishment
    Part 6 – Child safety orders

Children Act 2004

2004 Chapter 31

An Act to make provision for the establishment of a Children's Commissioner; to make provision about services provided to and for children and young people by local authorities and other persons; to make provision in relation to Wales about advisory and support services relating to family proceedings; to make provision about private fostering, child minding and day care, adoption review panels, the defence of reasonable punishment, the making of grants as respects children and families, child safety orders, the Children's Commissioner for Wales, the publication of material relating to children involved in certain legal proceedings and the disclosure by the Inland Revenue of information relating to children. [15th November 2004]

Be it enacted by the Queen's most Excellent Majesty, by and with the advice and consent of the Lords Spiritual and Temporal, and Commons, in this present Parliament assembled, and by the authority of the same, as follows:–

Part 1 Children's Commissioner

Establishes the Children's Commissioner, sets out the Commissioner's functions and the relationship with the Commissioners in Wales, Scotland and Northern Ireland. Makes clear that the Commissioner has jurisdiction in Wales, Scotland and Northern Ireland on matters not devolved from the UK Parliament.

1 Establishment

(1) There is to be an office of Children's Commissioner.

Establishes the office of Children's Commissioner.

(2) Schedule 1 has effect with respect to the Children's Commissioner.

Schedule 1 (p. 90) to the Act contains the legal status, general powers, tenure and remuneration, etc. of the Commissioner.

2 General function

(1) The Children's Commissioner has the function of promoting awareness of the views and interests of children in England.

The principal function of the Commissioner is to promote awareness of the 'views and interests' of children in England. A government defeat in the Lords to emphasise 'rights' rather than 'views and interests' was reversed in the Commons. However, in determining the 'interests' of children, the Commissioner has to take account of the UNCRC (Office of High Commissioner for Human Rights, 2004). See s. 2(11).

(2) The Children's Commissioner may in particular under this section–
 (a) encourage persons exercising functions or engaged in activities affecting children to take account of their views and interests;
 (b) advise the Secretary of State on the views and interests of children;
 (c) consider or research the operation of complaints procedures so far as relating to children;
 (d) consider or research any other matter relating to the interests of children;

The Commissioner has to
- *encourage persons working with children to take account of the views and interests of children*
- *advise the Secretary of State on the views and interests of children*
- *examine complaints procedures available to children*
- *investigate and publish findings about issues relating to children*

Plain guide to the Children Act 2004

(e) publish a report on any matter considered or researched by him under this section.

(3) The Children's Commissioner is to be concerned in particular under this section with the views and interests of children so far as relating to the following aspects of their well-being–
   (a) physical and mental health and emotional well-being;
   (b) protection from harm and neglect;
   (c) education, training and recreation;
   (d) the contribution made by them to society;
   (e) social and economic well-being.

	The Commissioner is directed to the 'five outcomes' for improving the well-being of children. See s. 10(2).

(4) The Children's Commissioner must take reasonable steps to involve children in the discharge of his function under this section, and in particular to–
   (a) ensure that children are made aware of his function and how they may communicate with him; and
   (b) consult children, and organisations working with children, on the matters he proposes to consider or research under subsection (2)(c) or (d).

Children must be central to the Commissioner's work. The Commissioner must make children aware of his/her functions and how children can communicate with him/her. The Commissioner must consult children and organisations working with children.

(5) Where the Children's Commissioner publishes a report under this section he must, if and to the extent that he considers it appropriate, also publish the report in a version which is suitable for children (or, if the report relates to a particular group of children, for those children).

Material produced by the Commissioner must take account of the level of understanding of children.

(6) The Children's Commissioner must for the purposes of subsection (4) have particular regard to groups of children who do not have other adequate means by which they can make their views known.

The Commissioner must pay particular regard to groups of children who do not have other means of making their views known. This is aimed at, for example, children in local authority care, asylum-seeker children etc. and other vulnerable groups of children whose views are not otherwise listened to.

(7) The Children's Commissioner is not under this section to conduct an investigation of the case of an individual child.

The Commissioner's investigatory powers relating to individual children can be found in ss. 3 to 7.

(8) The Children's Commissioner or a person authorised by him may for the purposes of his function under this section at any reasonable time–

The Commissioner, or somebody authorised by the Commissioner, has very wide powers to go into any premises (other than a private

(a) enter any premises, other than a private dwelling, for the purposes of interviewing any child accommodated or cared for there; and

(b) if the child consents, interview the child in private.

dwelling) to interview a child living there and to interview the child in private, if the child consents. The Commissioner will be able to go into residential schools and young offender institutions, for example.

(9) Any person exercising functions under any enactment must supply the Children's Commissioner with such information in that person's possession relating to those functions as the Children's Commissioner may reasonably request for the purposes of his function under this section (provided that the information is information which that person may, apart from this subsection, lawfully disclose to him).

Any body with statutory responsibilities relating to children must provide information to the Children's Commissioner on request. The body must hold the information. The request has to be reasonable and the body must be able to give the information legally. The term 'person' is used – this could enable the Commissioner to request information of an individual with statutory responsibilities such as a headteacher or a Director of Children's Services, although this is unlikely. Such a request would be to a school governing body or local authority.

(10) Where the Children's Commissioner has published a report under this section containing recommendations in respect of any person exercising functions under any enactment, he may require that person to state in writing, within such period as the Children's Commissioner may reasonably require, what action the person has taken or proposes to take in response to the recommendations.

Where the Commissioner has published a report on a general matter under s. 2(2)(e) that contains recommendations, the Commissioner may require any body with statutory responsibilities relating to children to state in writing within a reasonable period what the body intends to do to respond to the recommendations. See also s. 3(7).

(11) In considering for the purpose of his function under this section what constitutes the interests of children (generally or so far as relating to a particular matter) the Children's Commissioner must have regard to the United Nations Convention on the Rights of the Child.

The UNCRC is the international convention declaring the rights and interests of the child and the Commissioner must consider it when deciding what is in the interests of children.

(12) In subsection (11) the reference to the United Nations Convention on the Rights of the Child is to the Convention on the Rights of the Child adopted by the General Assembly of the United Nations on 20th November 1989, subject to any reservations, objec-

Any reference to the UNCRC is subject to any UK reservations to it. The two principal reservations relate to asylum-seeker children and young offenders.

plain guide to the Children Act 2004

tions or interpretative declarations by the United Kingdom for the time being in force.

3 Inquiries initiated by Commissioner

(1) Where the Children's Commissioner considers that the case of an individual child in England raises issues of public policy of relevance to other children, he may hold an inquiry into that case for the purpose of investigating and making recommendations about those issues.

The Commissioner may hold an inquiry into an individual case where such a case has wider implications for other children. The case must raise 'issues of public policy'. See s. 4(1).

(2) The Children's Commissioner may only conduct an inquiry under this section if he is satisfied that the inquiry would not duplicate work that is the function of another person (having consulted such persons as he considers appropriate).

The Commissioner must be satisfied that such an inquiry would not duplicate another body's work.

(3) Before holding an inquiry under this section the Children's Commissioner must consult the Secretary of State.

The Commissioner is required to consult the Secretary of State, but the Secretary of State has no power to veto a proposed inquiry.

(4) The Children's Commissioner may, if he thinks fit, hold an inquiry under this section, or any part of it, in private.

Inquiries can be held in private.

(5) As soon as possible after completing an inquiry under this section the Children's Commissioner must–
   (a) publish a report containing his recommendations; and
   (b) send a copy to the Secretary of State.

The Commissioner must publish a report containing recommendations as soon as possible after each inquiry and send a copy to the Secretary of State.

(6) The report need not identify any individual child if the Children's Commissioner considers that it would be undesirable for the identity of the child to be made public.

The Commissioner may protect the identity of a child involved in an inquiry.

(7) Where the Children's Commissioner has published a report under this section containing recommendations in respect of any person exercising functions under any enactment, he may require that person to state in writing, within such period as the Children's Commissioner may reasonably require, what action the person has taken or proposes to take in response to the recommendations.

The Commissioner can require a body with statutory responsibilities relating to children to respond in writing to any recommendations.

(8) Subsections (2) and (3) of section 250 of the Local Government Act 1972 (c. 70) apply for the purposes

The Commissioner has the power to summon people to give evi-

of an inquiry held under this section with the substitution for references to the person appointed to hold the inquiry of references to the Children's Commissioner.

	dence or documents, and to take evidence on oath. It is an offence not to comply. The Commissioner can direct parties to an inquiry to pay their own and/or other parties' costs.

4 Other inquiries held by Commissioner

(1) Where the Secretary of State considers that the case of an individual child in England raises issues of relevance to other children, he may direct the Children's Commissioner to hold an inquiry into that case.

The Secretary of State may direct the Commissioner to hold an inquiry into the case of an individual child if there are issues of relevance to other children. See s. 3(1).

(2) The Children's Commissioner may, if he thinks fit, hold an inquiry under this section, or any part of it, in private.

The Commissioner can decide to hold the inquiry, or any part of it, in private.

(3) The Children's Commissioner must, as soon as possible after the completion of an inquiry under this section, make a report in relation to the inquiry and send a copy to the Secretary of State.

The Commissioner must send a report of the inquiry as soon as possible to the Secretary of State.

(4) The Secretary of State must, subject to subsection (5), publish each report received by him under this section as soon as possible.

The Secretary of State must publish each report subject to s. 4(5).

(5) Where a report made under this section identifies an individual child and the Secretary of State considers that it would be undesirable for the identity of the child to be made public-
 (a) the Secretary of State may make such amendments to the report as are necessary to protect the identity of the child and publish the amended report only; or
 (b) if he considers that it is not possible to publish the report without identifying the child, he need not publish the report.

The Secretary of State can amend a Commissioner's report in order to protect the identity of a child. If the Secretary of State considers it impossible to publish the report without identifying the child, the report need not be published.

(6) The Secretary of State must lay a copy of each report published by him under this section before each House of Parliament.

The Secretary of State must present each report to Parliament.

(7) Subsections (2) to (5) of section 250 of the Local Government Act 1972 (c. 70) apply for the purposes of an inquiry held under this section.

The Commissioner has power to summon people to give evidence or documents and to take evidence on oath. It is an offence not to comply. The Secretary of State can direct

5 Functions of Commissioner in Wales

(1) The Children's Commissioner has the function of promoting awareness of the views and interests of children in Wales, except in so far as relating to any matter falling within the remit of the Children's Commissioner for Wales under section 72B, 73 or 74 of the Care Standards Act 2000 (c. 14).

parties to an inquiry to pay their own and/or other parties' costs.

Welsh issues not within the competence of the Children's Commissioner for Wales, that is 'non-devolved' matters, are the responsibility of the Children's Commissioner. Thus a child in Wales may have to look to the Children's Commissioner and not the Children's Commissioner for Wales on, for example, an issue to do with youth justice.

(2) Subsections (2) to (12) of section 2 apply in relation to the function of the Children's Commissioner under subsection (1) above as in relation to his function under that section.

For work in Wales, the Children's Commissioner's general functions are set out in s. 2.

(3) In discharging his function under subsection (1) above the Children's Commissioner must take account of the views of, and any work undertaken by, the Children's Commissioner for Wales.

The Children's Commissioner must take account of the views and work of the Children's Commissioner for Wales in relation to Welsh matters.

(4) Where the Children's Commissioner considers that the case of an individual child in Wales raises issues of public policy of relevance to other children, other than issues relating to a matter referred to in subsection (1) above, he may hold an inquiry into that case for the purpose of investigating and making recommendations about those issues.

The Children's Commissioner can hold an inquiry into the case of an individual child in Wales if there are issues of public policy and the issues do not fall within the remit of the Children's Commissioner for Wales.

(5) Subsections (2) to (8) of section 3 apply in relation to an inquiry under subsection (4) above.

The arrangements for Commissioner-initiated inquiries under s. 5(4) are the same as for England.

(6) Where the Secretary of State considers that the case of an individual child in Wales raises issues of relevance to other children, other than issues relating to matter referred to in subsection (1) above, he may direct the Children's Commissioner to hold an inquiry into that case.

The Secretary of State may direct the Children's Commissioner to hold an inquiry into the case of an individual child if there are issues of relevance to other children and the issues do not fall within the remit of the Children's Commissioner for Wales.

(7) Subsections (2) to (7) of section 4 apply in relation to an inquiry under subsection (6) above.

The arrangements for Commissioner-initiated inquiries

6 Functions of Commissioner in Scotland

(1) The Children's Commissioner has the function of promoting awareness of the views and interests of children in Scotland in relation to reserved matters.

Scottish issues not within the competence of the Commissioner for Children and Young People in Scotland, that is 'reserved' matters, are the responsibility of the Children's Commissioner. Thus a child in Scotland may have to look to the Children's Commissioner and not the Commissioner for Children and Young People in Scotland. For example, an issue to do with the asylum-seeker children in Scotland may fall within the remit of the Children's Commissioner.

(2) Subsections (2) to (12) of section 2 apply in relation to the function of the Children's Commissioner under subsection (1) above as in relation to his function under that section.

For work in Scotland, the Children's Commissioner's general functions are set out in s. 2.

(3) In discharging his function under subsection (1) above the Children's Commissioner must take account of the views of, and any work undertaken by, the Commissioner for Children and Young People in Scotland.

The Children's Commissioner must take account of the views and work of the Commissioner for Children and Young People in Scotland in relation to Scottish matters.

(4) Where the Children's Commissioner considers that the case of an individual child in Scotland raises issues of public policy of relevance to other children in relation to a reserved matter, he may hold an inquiry into that case for the purpose of investigating and making recommendations about those issues.

The Children's Commissioner can hold an inquiry into the case of an individual child in Scotland if there are issues of public policy and the issues do not fall within the remit of the Commissioner for Children and Young People in Scotland.

(5) Subsections (2) to (7) of section 3 apply in relation to an inquiry under subsection (4) above.

The arrangements for Children's Commissioner-initiated inquiries under s. 6(4) are similar to those for England except for the statutory basis of inquiries. See s. 6(6).

(6) Subsections (3) to (5) of section 210 of the Local Government (Scotland) Act 1973 (c. 65) apply for the purposes of an inquiry under subsection (4) above with the substitution of references to the Children's

The statutory basis of public inquiries under s. 6(5) in Scotland.

under s. 5(6) are the same as for England.

Commissioner for references to the person appointed to hold the inquiry.

(7) Where the Secretary of State considers that the case of an individual child in Scotland raises issues of relevance to other children in relation to a reserved matter, he may direct the Children's Commissioner to hold an inquiry into that case.

> The Secretary of State may direct the Children's Commissioner to hold an inquiry into the case of an individual child if there are issues of relevance to other children and the issues do not fall within the remit of the Commissioner for Children and Young People in Scotland.

(8) Subsections (2) to (6) of section 4 apply in relation to an inquiry under subsection (7) above.

> The arrangements for Commissioner-initiated inquiries under s. 6(7) are similar to those for England.

(9) Subsections (3) to (8) of section 210 of the Local Government (Scotland) Act 1973 apply for the purposes of an inquiry under subsection (7) above with the substitution (notwithstanding the provisions of section 53 of the Scotland Act 1998 (c. 46) (general transfer of functions to the Scottish Ministers)) of references to the Secretary of State for references to the Minister.

> The statutory basis of public inquiries under s. 6(7) in Scotland.

(10) In this section, "reserved matter" has the same meaning as in the Scotland Act 1998 (see section 30 of and Schedule 5 to that Act).

> The statutory derivation of 'reserved matter': those issues relating to Scotland that remain the responsibility of the UK Parliament; the most important for children relate to employment and immigration issues.

7 Functions of Commissioner in Northern Ireland

(1) The Children's Commissioner has the function of promoting awareness of the views and interests of children in Northern Ireland in relation to excepted matters.

> Northern Irish issues not within the competence of the Commissioner for Children and Young People for Northern Ireland, that is 'excepted' matters, are the responsibility of the Children's Commissioner. Thus a child in Northern Ireland may have to look to the Children's Commissioner and not the Commissioner for Children and Young People for Northern Ireland. For example, an issue to do with asylum-seeker children in Northern

	Ireland may fall within the remit of the Children's Commissioner.
(2) Subsections (2) to (12) of section 2 apply in relation to the function of the Children's Commissioner under subsection (1) above as in relation to his function under that section.	For work in Northern Ireland, the Children's Commissioner's general functions are set out in s. 2.
(3) In discharging his function under subsection (1) above the Children's Commissioner must take account of the views of, and any work undertaken by, the Commissioner for Children and Young People for Northern Ireland.	The Children's Commissioner must take account of the views and work of the Commissioner for Children and Young People for Northern Ireland in relation to Northern Irish matters.
(4) Where the Children's Commissioner considers that the case of an individual child in Northern Ireland raises issues of public policy which are of relevance to other children in relation to an excepted matter, he may hold an inquiry into that case for the purpose of investigating and making recommendations about those issues.	The Children's Commissioner can hold an inquiry into the case of an individual child in Northern Ireland if there are issues of public policy and the issues do not fall within the remit of the Commissioner for Children and Young People for Northern Ireland.
(5) Subsections (2) to (7) of section 3 apply in relation to an inquiry under subsection (4) above.	The arrangements for Commissioner-initiated inquiries under s. 7(4) are similar to those for England except for the statutory basis of inquiries. See s. 7(6).
(6) Paragraphs 2 to 5 of Schedule 8 to the Health and Personal Social Services (Northern Ireland) Order 1972 (S.I. 1972/1265 (N.I.14)) apply for the purposes of an inquiry under subsection (4) above with the substitution of references to the Children's Commissioner for references to the person appointed to hold the inquiry.	The statutory basis of public inquiries under s. 7(5) in Northern Ireland.
(7) Where the Secretary of State considers that the case of an individual child in Northern Ireland raises issues of relevance to other children in relation to an excepted matter, he may direct the Children's Commissioner to hold an inquiry into that case.	The Secretary of State may direct the Children's Commissioner to hold an inquiry into the case of an individual child if there are issues of relevance to other children and the issues do not fall within the remit of the Commissioner for Children and Young People for Northern Ireland.

(8) Subsections (2) to (6) of section 4 apply in relation to an inquiry under subsection (7) above.

The arrangements for Commissioner-initiated inquiries under s. 7(7) are similar to those for England.

(9) Paragraphs 2 to 8 of Schedule 8 to the Health and Personal Social Services (Northern Ireland) Order 1972 (S.I. 1972/1265 (N.I.14)) apply for the purposes of an inquiry under subsection (7) above with the substitution of references to the Secretary of State for references to the Ministry.

The statutory basis of public inquiries under s. 7(7) in Northern Ireland.

(10) In this section, "excepted matter" has the same meaning as in the Northern Ireland Act 1998 (c. 47).

The statutory derivation of 'excepted matter': those issues relating to Northern Ireland that remain the responsibility of the UK Parliament; the most important for children relate to immigration issues.

8 Annual reports

(1) As soon as possible after the end of each financial year the Children's Commissioner must make a report on-
   (a) the way in which he has discharged his functions under this Part, other than functions of holding inquiries;
   (b) what he has found in the course of exercising those functions during the year; and
   (c) the matters he intends to consider or research in the next financial year.

The Children's Commissioner is required to produce a detailed Annual Report of his/her activities in the past year, including findings and an outline of proposed activities.

(2) The Children's Commissioner must in particular under subsection (1)(a) include an account of the steps taken by him to involve in the discharge of the functions referred to in that provision the children in relation to whom those functions are exercised.

The Annual Report must state how children have been involved in the Commissioner's work.

(3) Where the Children's Commissioner makes a report under this section-
   (a) he must send a copy to the Secretary of State; and
   (b) the Secretary of State must as soon as possible lay a copy before each House of Parliament.

The report must be submitted to the Secretary of State.

(4) The Children's Commissioner must publish a report under this section as soon as possible after the Secretary of State has laid it before each House of Parliament.

Once the Secretary of State has submitted the report to Parliament, it is the Commissioner's responsibility to publish and disseminate the report.

(5) The Children's Commissioner must also, to the extent that he considers appropriate, publish any report made under this section in a version which is suitable for children.

A child-friendly version of the report must be produced.

(6) In this section, "financial year" has the same meaning as in paragraph 8 of Schedule 1.

The Commissioner's financial year runs from 1 April to 31 March each year.

9 Care leavers and young persons with learning disabilities

(1) This section applies for the purposes of this Part, other than section 2(11) and (12).

The Commissioner is not under a duty to have regard to the UNCRC (under s. 2(11) and 2(12)) when dealing with young people aged 18 years or older who are care leavers or who have learning disabilities.

(2) Any reference to a child includes, in addition to a person under the age of 18, a person aged 18, 19 or 20 who-
   (a) has been looked after by a local authority at any time after attaining the age of 16; or
   (b) has a learning disability.

Extends the remit of the Commissioner to young people who are 18 years and older but under 21 years, provided that they have been looked after by a local authority after attaining the age of 16 years or have a learning disability. See subsection (3) for definition of 'learning disability'.

(3) For the purposes of subsection (2)–
   a person is "looked after by a local authority" if–
      (a) for the purposes of the Children Act 1989 (c. 41), he is looked after by a local authority in England and Wales;
      (b) for the purposes of the Children (Scotland) Act 1995 (c. 36), he is looked after by a local authority in Scotland;
      (c) for the purposes of the Children (Northern Ireland) Order 1995 (S.I.1995/755 (N.I.2)), he is looked after by an authority in Northern Ireland;
   "learning disability" means a state of arrested or incomplete development of mind which induces significant impairment of intelligence and social functioning.

Defines a looked-after child in each part of the United Kingdom and 'learning disability'.

Part 2   Children's Services in England

Legislation to implement proposals in the Green Paper Every Child Matters are contained in this Part. The changes are aimed at supporting better integrated planning, commissioning and delivery of children's services, and provide for clear accountability.

General

Sections 10 to 12 describe how the public, voluntary and private bodies, which have responsibility for children, must cooperate to safeguard and promote the welfare of children, and share information about children.

10   Co-operation to improve well-being

It is expected that the 'duty to cooperate' will commence on 1 April 2005.

(1) Each children's services authority in England must make arrangements to promote co-operation between-
   (a) the authority;
   (b) each of the authority's relevant partners; and
   (c) such other persons or bodies as the authority consider appropriate, being persons or bodies of any nature who exercise functions or are engaged in activities in relation to children in the authority's area.

Each CSA, defined in s. 65, is given the duty of promoting cooperation between itself, 'relevant partners' (see subsection (4)) and other appropriate persons or bodies. Although the latter are not defined, Ministerial statements in Parliamentary debate suggest that CSAs should involve voluntary bodies and schools, and other bodies, including parent groups, working with children in the local authority area.

(2) The arrangements are to be made with a view to improving the well-being of children in the authority's area so far as relating to-
   (a) physical and mental health and emotional well-being;
   (b) protection from harm and neglect;
   (c) education, training and recreation;
   (d) the contribution made by them to society;
   (e) social and economic well-being.

The arrangements made in subsection (1) must aim to improve the well-being of children. In particular, the arrangements should promote the 'five outcomes' in paragraphs (a) to (e). These derive from the consultation exercise with young people following the publication of Every Child Matters (HM Treasury, 2003) and are described in the Next Steps (DfES, 2004c) document, page 25, as:

- be healthy: enjoying good physical and mental health and living a healthy lifestyle
- stay safe: being protected from harm and neglect and growing up able to look after themselves
- enjoy and achieve: getting the most out of life and developing broad skills for adulthood
- make a positive contribution: to the community and to society and not engaging in antisocial or offending behaviour
- achieve economic well-being.

(3) In making arrangements under this section a children's services authority in England must have regard to the importance of parents and other persons caring for children in improving the well-being of children.

The CSA must recognise that parents and carers have an important role in improving the well-being of children.

(4) For the purposes of this section each of the following is a relevant partner of a children's services authority in England-
   (a) where the authority is a county council for an area for which there is also a district council, the district council;
   (b) the police authority and the chief officer of police for a police area any part of which falls within the area of the children's services authority;
   (c) a local probation board for an area any part of which falls within the area of the authority;
   (d) a youth offending team for an area any part of which falls within the area of the authority;
   (e) a Strategic Health Authority and Primary Care Trust for an area any part of which falls within the area of the authority;
   (f) a person providing services under section 114 of the Learning and Skills Act 2000 (c. 21) in any part of the area of the authority;
   (g) the Learning and Skills Council for England.

The relevant partners of CSAs in England are defined. Paragraph (a) makes clear that in shire county areas, the districts must be included in cooperation arrangements. It is also a reminder that the CSA is more than a local authority carrying out its education and children's social services functions: it includes all functions (where held) in particular, housing, leisure, recreation and play, libraries and development planning. However, the Director of Children's Services (see s.18) will only by statute have responsibility for education and children's social services; the local authority can add to these responsibilities.

The relevant partners include bodies at a commissioning and planning level such as the police authority, the local authority in relation to schools, the SHA and PCT in relation to NHS Trusts, the PCT in relation to general practitioners, and the LSC in relation to further education and work-based learn-

plain guide to the Children Act 2004

ing. Other relevant partners include direct service providers, for example the local authority in relation to children's social services, the chief officer of police, the local probation board, the youth offending team, the PCT as a provider of community child health services and the Connexions service (under paragraph (f)).

The absence of a duty on head-teachers and school governing bodies, general practitioners and social housing landlords was debated at length in Parliament. The Government remained adamant that these bodies should be involved in the new arrangements through local leadership and not through legislative imposition.

(5) The relevant partners of a children's services authority in England must cooperate with the authority in the making of arrangements under this section.

Relevant partners must cooperate with the CSA in the making of arrangements to improve the well-being of children.

(6) A children's services authority in England and any of their relevant partners may for the purposes of arrangements under this section-
   (a) provide staff, goods, services, accommodation or other resources;
   (b) establish and maintain a pooled fund.

Provides the legislative basis for Children's Trusts. It enables Trusts to be established by the relevant partners by pooling funds and providing staff, goods, services, accommodation or other resources. The Government's target is that most local authorities will have a Children's Trust by 2006 and all by 2008.

(7) For the purposes of subsection (6) a pooled fund is a fund-
   (a) which is made up of contributions by the authority and the relevant partner or partners concerned; and
   (b) out of which payments may be made towards expenditure incurred in the discharge of functions of the authority and functions of the relevant partner or partners.

Defines the pooled fund mentioned in subsection (6)

(8) A children's services authority in England and each of their relevant partners must in exercising their functions under this section have regard to any guidance given to them for the purpose by the Secretary of State.

The CSA and relevant partners must 'have regard to' any guidance issued by the Secretary of State on the duty to cooperate to improve well-being. Draft statutory guidance was issued in December 2004 for final publication by 31 March 2005 (DfES, 2004a). The Explanatory Notes state that the guidance will set out the outcomes of cooperation, namely: effective working together to understand the needs of local children, agreeing the contribution each agency should make to meet those needs, effective sharing of information at a strategic level and about individual children to support multi-agency working, and oversight of arrangements for agencies to work together in integrated planning, commissioning and delivery of services as appropriate. Integrated commissioning in delivery of children's services should be considered.

(9) Arrangements under this section may include arrangements relating to-
(a) persons aged 18 and 19;
(b) persons over the age of 19 who are receiving services under sections 23C to 24D of the Children Act 1989 (c. 41);
(c) persons over the age of 19 but under the age of 25 who have a learning difficulty, within the meaning of section 13 of the Learning and Skills Act 2000, and are receiving services under that Act.

A 'child' is defined in s. 65 using the standard definition, namely a person under the age of 18. Several services, for example, school and college education and the Connexions service, are provided to 18 and 19 year-olds. This subsection enables appropriate services to continue to be provided once young people become adults in law. It also enables the cooperation arrangements for young people leaving care to continue past the age of 19 and also for young people with learning difficulties between the ages of 19 and 25.

11 Arrangements to safeguard and promote welfare

(1) This section applies to each of the following-
   (a) a children's services authority in England;
   (b) a district council which is not such an authority;
   (c) a Strategic Health Authority;
   (d) a Special Health Authority, so far as exercising functions in relation to England, designated by order made by the Secretary of State for the purposes of this section;
   (e) a Primary Care Trust;
   (f) an NHS trust all or most of whose hospitals, establishments and facilities are situated in England;
   (g) an NHS foundation trust;
   (h) the police authority and chief officer of police for a police area in England;
   (i) the British Transport Police Authority, so far as exercising functions in relation to England;
   (j) a local probation board for an area in England;
   (k) a youth offending team for an area in England;
   (l) the governor of a prison or secure training centre in England (or, in the case of a contracted out prison or secure training centre, its director);
   (m) any person to the extent that he is providing services under section 114 of the Learning and Skills Act 2000 (c. 21).

(2) Each person and body to whom this section applies must make arrangements for ensuring that-
   (a) their functions are discharged having regard to the need to safeguard and promote the welfare of children; and
   (b) any services provided by another person pursuant to arrangements made by the person or body in the discharge of their functions are provided having regard to that need.

(3) In the case of a children's services authority in England, the reference in subsection (2) to functions of the authority does not include functions to which section 175 of the Education Act 2002 (c. 32) applies.

It is expected that the duty to safeguard will commence on 1 October 2005.

The duty to safeguard and promote the welfare of all children is given to a wide range of bodies. Section 175 of the Education Act 2002 gives a similar duty to local education authorities and the governing bodies of maintained schools and further education colleges. Local authorities have long had a social services general duty to safeguard and promote the welfare of children within their area who are in need and a specific duty in respect of looked-after children (ss 17 and 22 of Children Act 1989 respectively). The list is similar to the 'relevant partners' of s. 7 with the addition of NHS trusts, a device to include NHS Direct (as a Special Health Authority), the British Transport Police and prisons and secure training establishments.

Each body mentioned in subsection (1) must carry out its functions having regard to the need to safeguard and promote the welfare of children. Paragraph (b) makes clear that the duty extends to contracted services, which covers services where privatised and also services which have historically been contracted, such as the general practitioners service.

Section 175 of the 2002 Act already places a duty on the LEA to safeguard and promote the welfare of children and have regard to guidance. DfES guidance was issued in September 2004:

(4) Each person and body to whom this section applies must in discharging their duty under this section have regard to any guidance given to them for the purpose by the Secretary of State.

12 Information databases

(1) The Secretary of State may for the purpose of arrangements under section 10 or 11 above or under section 175 of the Education Act 2002-
   (a) by regulations require children's services authorities in England to establish and operate databases containing information in respect of persons to whom such arrangements relate;
   (b) himself establish and operate, or make arrangements for the operation and establishment of, one or more databases containing such information.

Safeguarding Children in Education (DfES, 2004e). The LEA, as a local authority, is also the CSA as defined by s. 65(1). This subsection means that the s.175 duty applies to a CSA's education functions and the s.11 duty (of the Children Act 2004) applies to non-education functions.

The subsection (1) bodies must take account of statutory guidance. Draft guidance was published in December 2004 and it is expected that the final guidance will be published in May 2005.

The Green Paper Every Child Matters proposed improvements to information sharing between professionals working with children so that they are able to provide children and their families with the help and support they need at the earliest opportunity. This was supported in consultation provided that confidentiality of children and data protection could be guaranteed. See the Next Steps document paragraphs 2.36 to 2.40 (DfES, 2004c). It is expected that this section will commence in 2006 or 2007.

Regulations made by the affirmative resolution procedure (see s. 66(3)) can require CSAs to establish and operate information databases 'in respect of persons'. Alternatively, the Secretary of State may establish, or make arrangements for another body to establish, one or more databases containing information.

Importantly, the databases and their use must be used to help the CSA, relevant partners and other bodies

(2) The Secretary of State may for the purposes of arrangements under subsection (1)(b) by regulations establish a body corporate to establish and operate one or more databases.

(3) A database under this section may only include information falling within subsection (4) in relation to a person to whom arrangements specified in subsection (1) relate.

(4) The information referred to in subsection (3) is information of the following descriptions in relation to a person-
   (a) his name, address, gender and date of birth;
   (b) a number identifying him;
   (c) the name and contact details of any person with parental responsibility for him (within the meaning of section 3 of the Children Act 1989 (c. 41)) or who has care of him at any time;
   (d) details of any education being received by him (including the name and contact details of any educational institution attended by him);
   (e) the name and contact details of any person providing primary medical services in relation to him under Part 1 of the National Health Service Act 1977 (c. 49);

---

to carry out their duties to cooperate, and safeguard and promote the welfare of children, under ss. 10 or 11 of the Children Act 2004 or s.175 of the Education Act 2002.

If the Secretary of State decides to ask another body to operate the databases, regulations must establish a corporate body to carry out the task, i.e. this effectively limits the body to the public sector and could be a non-departmental public body similar to the NCSL or a public sector company like the Student Loans Company.

A child's details can only be placed on a database if a body with a duty to safeguard and promote the welfare of children holds the information. In practice, this will include virtually all children, as PCTs will hold information on live births received from a local authority's Registrar of Births, Marriages and Deaths. Children not born in England can be recorded when seeking services, e.g. education or primary health care.

Information that the database can contain is prescribed in this subsection and includes basic identifying information (name, gender, date of birth), a unique number, parental information, the provision of the basic universal services of education and primary health care, the provision of specialist services to be defined in regulations, and whether a practitioner has a cause for concern about the child. Other information can be added by regulations, but paragraph (h) excludes the inclusion of case notes and case histories. The DfES published Information sharing databases in children's services: consultation on

(f) the name and contact details of any person providing to him services of such description as the Secretary of State may by regulations specify;
(g) information as to the existence of any cause for concern in relation to him;
(h) information of such other description, not including medical records or other personal records, as the Secretary of State may by regulations specify.

recording practitioner details for potentially sensitive services and recording concern about the child or young person (DfES, 2004d) on 27 Oct 2004. Views are sought about how users of sensitive services, particularly targeted services, such as sexual health services, should be recorded and how practitioners should indicate a concern under paragraph (g) of this subsection.

(5) The Secretary of State may by regulations make provision in relation to the establishment and operation of any database or databases under this section.

The Secretary of State may by regulations (see s. 66(3)) provide for the establishment, management and operation of any database or databases.

(6) Regulations under subsection (5) may in particular make provision-
(a) as to the information which must or may be contained in any database under this section (subject to subsection (3));
(b) requiring a person or body specified in subsection (7) to disclose information for inclusion in the database;
(c) permitting a person or body specified in subsection (8) to disclose information for inclusion in the database;
(d) permitting or requiring the disclosure of information included in any such database;
(e) permitting or requiring any person to be given access to any such database for the purpose of adding or reading information;
(f) as to the conditions on which such access must or may be given;
(g) as to the length of time for which information must or may be retained;
(h) as to procedures for ensuring the accuracy of information included in any such database;
(i) in a case where a database is established by virtue of subsection (1)(b), requiring children's services authorities in England to participate in the operation of the database.

A list of issues that might be covered in the regulations made under subsection (5) includes requiring or permitting specified persons or bodies to disclose information to the database, requiring or permitting any person to be given access to the database for adding or retrieving information, the length of time that information can be included on a database and procedures for checking the accuracy of information on a database. Should the Secretary of State decide to establish a national database or databases, CSAs can be required to participate in the operation of such databases. The DfES consultation referred to in subsection (4) also discusses recording and accessing information.

(7) The persons and bodies referred to in subsection (6)(b) are-

Lists bodies that can be required to disclose information to a database.

(a) the persons and bodies specified in section 11(1);
(b) the Learning and Skills Council for England;
(c) the governing body of a maintained school in England (within the meaning of section 175 of the Education Act 2002 (c. 32));
(d) the governing body of an institution in England within the further education sector (within the meaning of that section);
(e) the proprietor of an independent school in England (within the meaning of the Education Act 1996 (c. 56));
(f) a person or body of such other description as the Secretary of State may by regulations specify.

These are both the providers of universal services under s.11 (the CSAs, Connexions services, police and PCTs) and the LSC, maintained school governing bodies, further education colleges and proprietors of independent schools.

(8) The persons and bodies referred to in subsection (6)(c) are-
(a) a person registered in England for child minding or the provision of day care under Part 10A of the Children Act 1989 (c. 41);
(b) a voluntary organisation exercising functions or engaged in activities in relation to persons to whom arrangements specified in subsection (1) relate;
(c) the Commissioners of Inland Revenue;
(d) a registered social landlord;
(e) a person or body of such other description as the Secretary of State may by regulations specify.

Lists bodies that are permitted to disclose information to a database, including childminders and day-care providers, voluntary organisations, the Inland Revenue, and registered social landlords.

(9) The Secretary of State may provide information for inclusion in a database under this section.

Government departments may supply information, for example benefit records from the DWP.

(10) The provision which may be made under subsection (6)(e) includes provision for a person of a description specified in the regulations to determine what must or may be done under the regulations.

Regulations may allow for the delegation of decisions about whether to give a person access to the database to the person or body (Secretary of State, corporate body or CSA) who has established the database.

(11) Regulations under subsection (5) may also provide that anything which may be done under regulations under subsection (6)(c) to (e) or (9) may be done notwithstanding any rule of common law which prohibits or restricts the disclosure of information.

Allows common law requirements on the disclosure of information to be overridden by permitted persons or bodies providing information to, or accessing information from, a database.

(12) Any person or body establishing or operating a database under this section must in the establishment or

Database operators must comply with any direction of the Secretary of

operation of the database have regard to any guidance, and comply with any direction, given to that person or body by the Secretary of State.

(13) Guidance or directions under subsection (12) may in particular relate to-
   (a) the management of a database under this section;
   (b) the technical specifications for any such database;
   (c) the security of any such database;
   (d) the transfer and comparison of information between databases under this section;
   (e) the giving of advice in relation to rights under the Data Protection Act 1998 (c. 29).

Local Safeguarding Children Boards

13 Establishment of LSCBs

(1) Each children's services authority in England must establish a Local Safeguarding Children Board for their area.

(2) A Board established under this section must include such representative or representatives of-
   (a) the authority by which it is established, and
   (b) each Board partner of that authority, as the Secretary of State may by regulations prescribe.

State about the operation of a database and have regard to statutory guidance, e.g. data security.

Lists matters that can be the subject of a direction or guidance under subsection (12) clearly indicating that directions must be related to technical, security and operational issues, including subject rights under the Data Protection Act 1998.

The Act requires each CSA to establish a LSCB. The LSCB is a statutory body which is charged with ensuring the effectiveness of local arrangements and services to safeguard children, including services provided by individual agencies. It will be the main mechanism by which the CSA can make the other partners accountable for the provision of services to children. The Boards will replace the non-statutory ACPCs. See the Next Steps document (DfES, 2004c) paragraphs 2.15 to 2.18.

It is expected that LSCBs will commence on 1 April 2006 and statutory guidance under s. 16(2) will be available in December 2005.

Each CSA must to set up a LSCB but see subsection (8).

Regulations will prescribe that the authority and each partner (see subsection (3)) must be represented on the LSCB. The wording allows a body to be represented by more than one representative or a representative could represent

plain guide to the Children Act 2004

(3) For the purposes of this section each of the following is a Board partner of a children's services authority in England-
   (a) where the authority is a county council for an area for which there is also a district council, the district council;
   (b) the chief officer of police for a police area any part of which falls within the area of the authority;
   (c) a local probation board for an area any part of which falls within the area of the authority;
   (d) a youth offending team for an area any part of which falls within the area of the authority;
   (e) a Strategic Health Authority and a Primary Care Trust for an area any part of which falls within the area of the authority;
   (f) an NHS trust and an NHS foundation trust all or most of whose hospitals, establishments and facilities are situated in the area of the authority;
   (g) a person providing services under section 114 of the Learning and Skills Act 2000 (c. 21) in any part of the area of the authority;
   (h) the Children and Family Court Advisory and Support Service;
   (i) the governor of any secure training centre in the area of the authority (or, in the case of a contracted out secure training centre, its director);
   (j) the governor of any prison in the area of the authority which ordinarily detains children (or, in the case of a contracted out prison, its director).

(4) A children's services authority in England must take reasonable steps to ensure that the Local Safeguarding Children Board established by them includes representatives of relevant persons and bodies of such descriptions as may be prescribed by the Secretary of State in regulations.

(5) A Local Safeguarding Children Board established under this section may also include representatives of such other relevant persons or bodies as the authority by which it is established consider, after consulting their Board partners, should be represented on it.

---

more than one body, as provided by regulations.

The bodies that must be represented on the LSCB are:
- CSA
- district councils in shire areas
- police force
- probation service
- youth offending team
- SHA and PCTs that cover any area of the CSA
- NHS trusts and NHS foundation trusts whose hospitals and facilities are situated in the area of the authority
- Connexions service
- CAFCASS
- secure training centres
- prisons that ordinarily detain children.

In addition to the membership prescribed by subsection (3), the Secretary of State can prescribe in regulations other relevant persons and bodies that the CSA must take reasonable steps to ensure are represented on the LSCB, for example schools and voluntary groups.

A CSA, after consulting the LSCB, can add representatives of other relevant persons or bodies to the Board.

(6) For the purposes of subsections (4) and (5), relevant persons and bodies are persons and bodies of any nature exercising functions or engaged in activities relating to children in the area of the authority in question.

> Representatives added to the Board by virtue of subsections (4) and (5) must be 'engaged in activities' with children in the area.

(7) In the establishment and operation of a Local Safeguarding Children Board under this section-
 (a) the authority establishing it must co-operate with each of their Board partners; and
 (b) each Board partner must co-operate with the authority.

> The CSA and the partners must cooperate in the establishment of the LSCB.

(8) Two or more children's services authorities in England may discharge their respective duties under subsection (1) by establishing a Local Safeguarding Children Board for their combined area (and where they do so, any reference in this section or sections 14 to 16 to the authority establishing the Board shall be read as a reference to the authorities establishing it).

> Two or more CSAs may establish a joint LSCB, although this seems an unlikely option for virtually all CSAs.

14 Functions and procedure of LSCBs

(1) The objective of a Local Safeguarding Children Board established under section 13 is-
 (a) to co-ordinate what is done by each person or body represented on the Board for the purposes of safeguarding and promoting the welfare of children in the area of the authority by which it is established; and
 (b) to ensure the effectiveness of what is done by each such person or body for those purposes.

> An LSCB must coordinate, and ensure the effectiveness of, the work of each body or person represented on the Board in safeguarding and promoting the welfare of children.

(2) A Local Safeguarding Children Board established under section 13 is to have such functions in relation to its objective as the Secretary of State may by regulations prescribe (which may in particular include functions of review or investigation).

> The Secretary of State may prescribe by regulations the functions of the LSCB, which will be largely based on the functions of the ACPC, as set out in Working Together to Safeguard Children (DoH, HO and DfEE, 1999).

(3) The Secretary of State may by regulations make provision as to the procedures to be followed by a Local Safeguarding Children Board established under section 13.

> The Secretary of State may prescribe by regulations the procedures of the LSCB, for example the keeping of a register of attendance.

15 Funding of LSCBs

(1) Any person or body specified in subsection (3) may make payments towards expenditure incurred by, or for purposes connected with, a Local Safeguarding Children Board established under section 13-
 (a) by making the payments directly; or
 (b) by contributing to a fund out of which the payments may be made.

LSCBs are funded by direct payments or by pooling funds from Board partners.

(2) Any person or body specified in subsection (3) may provide staff, goods, services, accommodation or other resources for purposes connected with a Local Safeguarding Children Board established under section 13.

Contributions may be in kind, in the form of staff, accommodation, etc.

(3) The persons and bodies referred to in subsections (1) and (2) are-
 (a) the children's services authority in England by which the Board is established;
 (b) any person who is a Board partner of the authority under section 13(3)(a) to (h);
 (c) in a case where the governor of a secure training centre or prison is a Board partner of the authority, the Secretary of State; and
 (d) in a case where the director of a contracted out secure training centre or prison is a Board partner of the authority, the contractor.

The contributors to the running costs are the CSA and Board partners. In the case of the governor of a secure training centre or prison, the Secretary of State is the contributor, although if the service has been contracted out, the contractor is the contributor.

16 LSCBs: supplementary

(1) The Secretary of State may by regulations make provision as to the functions of children's services authorities in England relating to Local Safeguarding Children Boards established by them.

The Secretary of State may prescribe by regulations the administrative and support services that CSAs must provide to LSCBs.

(2) A children's services authority in England and each of their Board partners must, in exercising their functions relating to a Local Safeguarding Children Board, have regard to any guidance given to them for the purpose by the Secretary of State.

The Secretary of State can issue statutory guidance to the CSA and Board partners about the operation of the LSCB, for example the funding and arrangements for investigating a child death. It is likely that guidance will be issued along the lines of paragraph 2.17 of the Next Steps document (DfES, 2004c) on chairing the LSCB: 'We would expect the Director of Children's Services to chair the Board unless

Local authority administration

it is considered more appropriate to have an independent chair.'

The Act requires changes in local authority administration. In particular, a Director of Children's Services must be appointed to carry out certain functions. A lead elected member for children must also be appointed. Local authority plannning duties are culled and replaced by a single CYPP.

17 Children and young people's plans

It is expected that the new planning duty will commence on 1 April 2006.

(1) The Secretary of State may by regulations require a children's services authority in England from time to time to prepare and publish a plan setting out the authority's strategy for discharging their functions in relation to children and relevant young persons.

Enables the Secretary of State to require by regulations each CSA to prepare and publish a strategic plan setting out how services for children and young people will be provided. Schedule 5, part 1 repeals the legislative basis of the following: children's services plan, behaviour support plan, class size reduction plan, education development plan, school organisation plan, early years development and childcare plan, and the adoption services plan. Draft DfES guidance (DfES, 2004a) is expected to be published in January 2005 and final guidance is expected to be published in April 2005. The guidance will not be statutory guidance.

(2) Regulations under this section may in particular make provision as to-
 (a) the matters to be dealt with in a plan under this section;
 (b) the period to which a plan under this section is to relate;
 (c) when and how a plan under this section must be published;
 (d) keeping a plan under this section under review;

Regulations can prescribe the content, timescale, publication and review of the CYPP, and the consultation required during the plan's preparation.

    (e) consultation to be carried out during preparation of a plan under this section.

(3) The matters for which provision may be made under subsection (2)(a) include in particular-
    (a) the arrangements made or to be made under section 10 by a children's services authority in England;
    (b) the strategy or proposals in relation to children and relevant young persons of any person or body with whom a children's services authority in England makes or proposes to make such arrangements.

> The regulations may require the cooperation arrangements made under s. 10 to be included in the plan and the strategic plans for children of other bodies. The Explanatory Notes indicate that children's health services, youth justice and services provided by the voluntary and community sector should be included in the plan and that consistency with the CYPP should be demonstrated.

(4) The power to make regulations conferred by this section shall, for the purposes of subsection (1) of section 100 of the Local Government Act 2003 (c. 26), be regarded as included among the powers mentioned in subsection (2) of that section.

> Enables 'excellent' local authorities as judged by the Comprehensive Performance Review to be relieved of all or part of the requirement to produce a CYPP. This subsection could also be used to require a poorly performing local authority to produce a more detailed plan.

(5) In this section "relevant young persons" means persons, other than children, in relation to whom arrangements under section 10 may be made.

> The CYPP covers the same group of young people as the duty to cooperate specifies in s. 10(9).

18 Director of children's services

(1) A children's services authority in England may, and with effect from the appointed day must, appoint an officer for the purposes of-
    (a) the functions conferred on or exercisable by the authority which are specified in subsection (2); and
    (b) such other functions conferred on or exercisable by the authority as may be prescribed by the Secretary of State by regulations.

> Each CSA may appoint an officer for 'the purposes of' the functions prescribed in subsection (2) and such other functions as prescribed in regulations. It is expected that this duty will commence on 1 April 2005. From this date, a CSA may appoint a director with the responsibilities under this section. From the 'appointed day', each CSA must have a director in post. It is expected that this date will be 1 April 2008.

(2) The functions referred to in subsection (1)(a) are-
    (a) functions conferred on or exercisable by the authority in their capacity as a local education

> The functions that the officer must be appointed 'for the purposes of'

authority;
(b) functions conferred on or exercisable by the authority which are social services functions (within the meaning of the Local Authority Social Services Act 1970 (c. 42)), so far as those functions relate to children;
(c) the functions conferred on the authority under sections 23C to 24D of the Children Act 1989 (c. 41) (so far as not falling within paragraph (b));
(d) the functions conferred on the authority under sections 10 to 12 and 17 of this Act; and (e) any functions exercisable by the authority under section 31 of the Health Act 1999 (c. 8) on behalf of an NHS body (within the meaning of that section), so far as those functions relate to children.

are the following, conferred on, or exercisable by, the local authority:
- *LEA*
- *social services that relate to children*
- *children leaving local authority care*
- *CSA as far as cooperation, safeguarding and promoting the welfare of children and information databases*
- *health services for children if transferred to the local authority.*

(3) Subsection (2)(a) does not include-
(a) functions under section 120(3) of the Education Reform Act 1988 (c. 40) (functions of LEAs with respect to higher and further education);
(b) functions under section 85(2) and (3) of the Further and Higher Education Act 1992 (c. 13) (finance and government of locally funded further and higher education);
(c) functions under section 15B of the Education Act 1996 (c. 56) or section 23 of the Learning and Skills Act 2000 (c. 21) (education for persons who have attained the age of 19);
(d) functions under section 22 of the Teaching and Higher Education Act 1998 (c. 30) (financial support to students);
(e) such other functions conferred on or exercisable by a children's services authority in England in their capacity as a local education authority as the Secretary of State may by regulations prescribe.

Remaining LEA functions relating to further and higher education and such other functions as the Secretary of State may prescribe are not the responsibility of the officer appointed under subsection (1). But see subsection (6).

(4) An officer appointed by a children's services authority in England under this section is to be known as their "director of children's services".

The officer appointed in subsection (1) must have the title 'director of children's services' (DCS).

(5) The director of children's services appointed by a children's services authority in England may also have responsibilities relating to such functions conferred on or exercisable by the authority, in addition to those specified in subsection (1), as the authority consider appropriate.

The DCS may have such additional responsibilities as determined by the CSA.

plain guide to the Children Act 2004

(6) The functions in relation to which a director of children's services may have responsibilities by virtue of subsection (5) include those referred to in subsection (3)(a) to (e).

The DCS may carry out the LEA functions listed in subsection (3) if determined by the CSA.

(7) A children's services authority in England must have regard to any guidance given to them by the Secretary of State for the purposes of this section.

The CSA must have regard to the guidance from the Secretary of State on the role and responsibilities of the DCS. The DfES Draft Statutory Guidance on the Role and Responsibilities of the Director of Children's Services and the Lead Member for Children's Services (DfES, 2004a) was issued on 26 November 2004 for response by 18 February 2005. It is expected that the final guidance will be published by 31 March 2005.

(8) Two or more children's services authorities in England may for the purposes of this section, if they consider that the same person can efficiently discharge, for both or all of them, the responsibilities of director of children's services, concur in the appointment of a person as director of children's services for both or all of them.

Two or more CSAs may appoint a joint DCS.

(9) The amendments in Schedule 2-
   (a) have effect, in relation to any authority which appoint a director of children's services before the appointed day, from the day of his appointment; and
   (b) on and after the appointed day have effect for all purposes.

Schedule 2, which makes changes to other legislation as a consequence of the appointment of the DCS, commences on the day the first DCS comes into post after the commencement of section 18. On, or after, the 'appointed day' schedule 2 has effect for all purposes.

(10) In this section, "the appointed day" means such day as the Secretary of State may by order appoint.

The Secretary of State determines the appointed day, expected to be 1 April 2008.

19 Lead member for children's services

(1) A children's services authority in England must, in making arrangements for the discharge of-
   (a) the functions conferred on or exercisable by the authority specified in section 18(1)(a) and (b), and

Each CSA must designate an elected 'lead member for children's services', but the member may have additional responsibilities. It is

(b) such other functions conferred on or exercisable by the authority as the authority consider appropriate, designate one of their members as their "lead member for children's services".

(2) A children's services authority in England must have regard to any guidance given to them by the Secretary of State for the purposes of subsection (1).

expected that this provision will commence on 1 April 2005.

The CSA must have regard to guidance from the Secretary of State on the roles and responsibilities of the lead member for children's services. See comment on s.18(7).

Inspections of children's services

In order to assess the effectiveness of children's services, the Act makes provision for JARs supported by a Framework for the Inspection of Children's Services in ss. 20 to 24 for England only.

The joint inspectorates' consultation on the Integrated Inspection Framework was launched in December 2004 and it is expected that the final Framework will be published in May 2005. The joint inspectorates' discussion paper Every child matters (Ofsted, 2004), which can be found on the Ofsted website, reports that trials of the new methodology began in late 2004 and that a three-year programme of JARs will start in Summer 2005.

20 Joint area reviews

(1) Any two or more of the persons and bodies to which this section applies must, at the request of the Secretary of State-
   (a) conduct, in accordance with a timetable drawn up by them and approved by the Secretary of State, a review of children's services provided in-
      (i) the area of every children's services authority in England;
      (ii) the areas of such children's services authorities in England as may be specified in the request;
   (b) conduct a review of such children's services provided in the area of such children's services authority in England as may be specified in the request.

The Secretary of State may request any two or more of the inspectorates to undertake JARs of children's services in every CSA. A request can be made to conduct JARs in some but not all CSAs. A request can also be made to conduct reviews of particular children's services in specified areas.

(2) Any two or more of the persons and bodies to which this section applies may conduct a review of any children's services provided in the area of a particular children's services authority in England.

Two or more inspectorates may undertake a review on their own initiative.

(3) The purpose of a review under this section is to evaluate the extent to which, taken together, the children's services being reviewed improve the well-being of children and relevant young persons (and in particular to evaluate how those services work together to improve their well-being).

The purpose of a review is defined. Reviews will focus on how services improve the well-being of children and how the providers work together.

(4) The persons and bodies to which this section applies are-
   (a) the Chief Inspector of Schools;
   (b) the Adult Learning Inspectorate;
   (c) the Commission for Social Care Inspection;
   (d) the Commission for Healthcare Audit and Inspection;
   (e) the Audit Commission for Local Authorities and the National Health Service in England and Wales;
   (f) the chief inspector of constabulary;
   (g) Her Majesty's Chief Inspector of the National Probation Service for England and Wales;
   (h) Her Majesty's Chief Inspector of Court Administration; and
   (i) the Chief Inspector of Prisons.

Lists the nine inspectorates involved. The joint inspectorates' discussion paper (Ofsted, 2004) listed a tenth inspectorate, HM Crown Prosecution Service Inspectorate. The formal names of the inspectorates are given: the Chief Inspector of Schools (HMCI) is known as Ofsted and the Commission for Health Care Audit and Inspection is known as the Healthcare Commission. The Commission for Social Care Inspection is a body formed in April 2004 from the Social Services Inspectorate and the social care functions of the National Care Standards Commission.

(5) Reviews under this section are to be conducted in accordance with arrangements made by the Chief Inspector of Schools.

Ofsted has responsibility for co-ordinating the process.

(6) Before making arrangements for the purposes of reviews under this section the Chief Inspector of Schools must consult such of the other persons and bodies to which this section applies as he considers appropriate.

Ofsted has to consult with the other inspectorates on the processes to be followed.

(7) The annual report of the Chief Inspector of Schools required by subsection (7)(a) of section 2 of the School Inspections Act 1996 (c. 57) to be made to the Secretary of State must include an account of reviews under this section; and the power conferred by subsection (7)(b) of that section to make other reports to the Secretary of State includes a power to make reports about such reviews.

Ofsted has to include an account of this element of the work in its annual report of Ofsted

(8) The Secretary of State may by regulations make provision for the purposes of reviews under this section and in particular provision-
   (a) requiring or facilitating the sharing or production of information for the purposes of a review under this section (including provision for the creation of criminal offences);
   (b) authorising any person or body conducting a review under this section to enter any premises for the purposes of the review (including provision for the creation of criminal offences);
   (c) imposing requirements as to the making of a report on each review under this section;
   (d) for the making by such persons as may be specified in or under the regulations of written statements of proposed action in the light of the report and the period within which any such action must or may be taken;
   (e) for the provision to members of the public of copies of reports and statements made under paragraphs (c) and (d), and for charging in respect of any such provision;
   (f) for the disapplication, in consequence of a requirement under this section, of any requirement under any other enactment to conduct an assessment or to do anything in connection with an assessment.

The Secretary of State may make regulations with regard to aspects of the review process, as set out here.

(9) Regulations under subsection (8) may in particular make provision by applying enactments falling within subsection (10), with or without modification, for the purposes of reviews under this section.

Technical provision required for subsection (10).

(10) The enactments falling within this subsection are enactments relating to the powers of persons and bodies to which this section applies for the purposes of assessments other than reviews under this section.

With subsection (9), enables inspectorates to contribute information collected for purposes other than JARs.

(11) Regulations under subsection (8) may make provision authorising or requiring the doing of anything by reference to the determination of a person of a description specified in the regulations.

This is a technical subsection.

21 Framework

(1) The Chief Inspector of Schools must devise a Framework for Inspection of Children's Services ("the Framework").

Ofsted must devise a framework for JARs.

(2) The Framework must, for the purpose specified in subsection (3), set out principles to be applied by any person or body conducting a relevant assessment.

	The framework must include a set of principles.

(3) The purpose referred to in subsection (2) is to ensure that relevant assessments properly evaluate and report on the extent to which children's services improve the well-being of children and relevant young persons.

	The principles must focus on the extent to which children's services improve the well-being of all children in the area.

(4) The principles in the Framework may-
 (a) include principles relating to the organisation of the results of any relevant assessment;
 (b) make different provision for different cases.

	The principles should include details of the way of structuring any report and should allow for differentiated inspections.

(5) For the purposes of subsections (2) to (4) a relevant assessment is an assessment conducted under any enactment in relation to any children's services.

	Establishes that an assessment must relate to children's services.

(6) When devising the Framework, the Chief Inspector of Schools must consult the other persons and bodies to which section 20 applies.

	Requires Ofsted to consult with all the other inspectorates in devising the framework.

(7) The Chief Inspector of Schools must publish the Framework, but before doing so must-
 (a) consult such persons and bodies, other than those referred to in subsection (6), as he thinks fit; and
 (b) obtain the consent of the Secretary of State.

	Requires Ofsted to publish the Framework and to consult widely on it and obtain the consent of the Secretary of State first.

(8) The Chief Inspector of Schools may at any time revise the Framework (and subsections (6) and (7) apply in relation to revisions to the Framework as to the original Framework).

	Allows Ofsted to revise the Framework, again subject to consultation with the other inspectorates and others and subject to the consent of the Secretary of State.

22 Co-operation and delegation

(1) Each person or body with functions under any enactment of conducting assessments of children's services must for the purposes of those assessments co-operate with other persons or bodies with such functions.

	All those involved in a JAR must cooperate with all others involved.

(2) A person or body with functions under any enactment of conducting assessments of children's services may delegate any of those functions to any other person or body with such functions.

	An inspectorate may delegate functions to another inspectorate.

23 Sections 20 to 22: interpretation

(1) This section applies for the purposes of sections 20 to 22.

A technical subsection, which introduces a number of definitions in subsections (2) to (5).

(2) "Assessment" includes an inspection, review, investigation or study.

'Assessment' is a generic term used for all the terms found in legislation to describe the activities of the inspectorates, namely: inspection, review, investigation or study.

(3) "Children's services" means-
   (a) anything done for or in relation to children and relevant young persons (alone or with other persons)-
      (i) in respect of which, apart from section 20, a person or body to which that section applies conducts any kind of assessment, or secures that any kind of assessment is conducted; and
      (ii) which is specified in, or is of a description prescribed by, regulations made by the Secretary of State;
   (b) any function under sections 10 and 13 to 19; and
   (c) any function conferred on a children's services authority under section 12.

The only definition of 'children's services' in the Act, although it only applies to JARs and the Framework for Inspection. A 'children's service' is a service that is assessed by one of the inspectorates. The Secretary of State can also define 'children's services' in regulations. Children's services are also defined in terms of the specified sections in Part 1 of the Act enabling, for example, JARs to assess CSA work on information sharing under s.12.

(4) "Relevant young persons" means persons, other than children, in relation to whom arrangements under section 10 may be made.

See subsection 10(9) for definition of relevant young people; 18 and 19 year-olds, etc. are included.

(5) "The Chief Inspector of Schools" means Her Majesty's Chief Inspector of Schools in England.

The Chief Inspector of Schools is the HMCI for England, i.e. the head of Ofsted.

24 Performance rating of social services

(1) In section 79(2) of the Health and Social Care (Community Health and Standards) Act 2003 (c.43) (duty of Commission for Social Care Inspection to award a performance rating to a local authority), for the words from "a performance rating" to the end substitute-
      "(a) a performance rating to that authority in respect of all the English local authority social services provided by, or pursuant to arrangements made by, that authority-

Amends the Health and Social Care (Community Health and Standards) Act 2003 to mean that the Commission for Social Care Inspection will, in future, award separate annual performance ratings for social services for children and care leavers, and for other social services, i.e. for adults.

   (i) to or so far as relating to persons under the age of eighteen; or
   (ii) under sections 23C to 24D of the Children Act 1989; and
  (b) a performance rating to that authority in respect of all other English local authority social services provided by, or pursuant to arrangements made by, that authority."

(2) In section 81(2) of that Act (duty of the Commission to inform the Secretary of State where it awards the lowest performance rating under section 79), for "section 79" substitute "section 79(2)(a) or (b)".

	A technical amendment to the Health and Social Care (Community Health and Standards) Act 2003.

Part 3   Children's Services In Wales

Similar provisions for Wales are made to those in Part 2. There is no equivalent legislation on the inspection of children's services, however.

General

These provisions are similar to the England provisions: s. 25 mirrors s. 10 on cooperation, s. 26 mirrors s. 17 on planning, s. 27 provides for management arrangements for local authorities and NHS bodies and has a similar function to ss. 18 and 19, s. 28 mirrors s.11 on safeguarding and promoting the welfare of children, and s. 29 mirrors s. 12 on information databases.

25 Co-operation to improve well-being: Wales

(1) Each children's services authority in Wales must make arrangements to promote co-operation between-
   (a) the authority;
   (b) each of the authority's relevant partners; and
   (c) such other persons or bodies as the authority consider appropriate, being persons or bodies of any nature who exercise functions or are engaged in activities in relation to children in the authority's area.

The CSA, defined in s. 65, is given the duty of promoting cooperation between itself, 'relevant partners' (see subsection (4)) and other appropriate persons or bodies. Although the latter are not defined, Ministerial statements in Parliamentary debate suggest that CSAs should involve voluntary bodies and schools, and other bodies, including parent groups, working with children in the local authority area.

(2) The arrangements are to be made with a view to improving the well-being of children in the authority's area so far as relating to-
   (a) physical and mental health and emotional well-being;
   (b) protection from harm and neglect;
   (c) education, training and recreation;
   (d) the contribution made by them to society;
   (e) social and economic well-being.

The arrangements made in subsection (1) must improve the well-being of children. In particular, the arrangements must promote the outcomes in paragraphs (a) to (e). See s.10(2) for more information.

(3) In making arrangements under this section a children's services authority in Wales must have regard to the importance of parents and other persons caring for children in improving the well-being of children.

The CSA must recognise that parents and carers have an important role in improving the well-being of children.

(4) For the purposes of this section each of the following is the relevant partner of a children's services authority in Wales-
- (a) the police authority and the chief officer of police for a police area any part of which falls within the area of the children's services authority;
- (b) a local probation board for an area any part of which falls within the area of the authority;
- (c) a youth offending team for an area any part of which falls within the area of the authority;
- (d) a Local Health Board for an area any part of which falls within the area of the authority;
- (e) an NHS trust providing services in the area of the authority;
- (f) the National Council for Education and Training for Wales.

The relevant partners are defined. The list is similar to that for England except that NHS Trusts are included, recognising the different organisation of NHS services in Wales. The Youth Support Service in Wales is a local government service and is not listed separately.

The absence of a duty on headteachers and school governing bodies, general practitioners and social housing landlords was debated at length in Parliament. The Government remained adamant that these bodies should be involved in the new arrangements through local leadership and not through legislative imposition.

(5) The relevant partners of a children's services authority in Wales must cooperate with the authority in the making of arrangements under this section.

Relevant partners must cooperate with the CSA in the making of arrangements to improve the well-being of children.

(6) A children's services authority in Wales and any of their relevant partners may for the purposes of arrangements under this section-
- (a) provide staff, goods, services, accommodation or other resources;
- (b) establish and maintain a pooled fund.

The partners are able to pool funds and provide staff, goods, services, accommodation and other resources. The Explanatory Note makes clear that there is no expectation that Children's Trusts will be created in Wales.

(7) For the purposes of subsection (6) a pooled fund is a fund-
- (a) which is made up of contributions by the authority and the relevant partner or partners concerned; and
- (b) out of which payments may be made towards expenditure incurred in the discharge of functions of the authority and functions of the relevant partner or partners.

Defines the pooled fund mentioned in subsection (6).

(8) A children's services authority in Wales and each of their relevant partners must in exercising their functions under this section have regard to any guidance given to them for the purpose by the Assembly.

The CSA and relevant partners must 'have regard to' any guidance issued by the Assembly on the duty to cooperate to improve well-being. The Assembly has announced that it intends to use statutory guidance to put on a statutory footing the established Children and Young People's Framework Partnerships and Children's Parnterships.

(9) The Assembly must obtain the consent of the Secretary of State before giving guidance under subsection (8) at any time after the coming into force of any of paragraphs (a) to (c) of subsection (4).

The Assembly must obtain the consent of the Secretary of State before issuing guidance to non-devolved bodies. This principally affects youth justice bodies.

(10) Arrangements under this section may include arrangements relating to-
   (a) persons aged 18 and 19;
   (b) persons over the age of 19 who are receiving-
      (i) services under sections 23C to 24D of the Children Act 1989 (c. 41); or
      (ii) youth support services (within the meaning of section 123 of the Learning and Skills Act 2000 (c. 21)).

A 'child' is defined in s. 65 using the standard definition, namely a person under the age of 18. Several services, for example school and college education, are provided to 18 and 19 year-olds. This subsection enables appropriate services to continue to be provided once young people become adults in law. It also enables the cooperation arrangements for young people leaving care to continue past the age of 19 and for young people involved in youth support services, that is young people under the of 26.

26 Children and young people's plans: Wales

(1) The Assembly may by regulations require a children's services authority in Wales from time to time to prepare and publish a plan setting out the authority's strategy for discharging their functions in relation to children and relevant young persons.

Enables the Assembly to require by regulations each CSA to prepare and publish a strategic plan setting out how services for children and young people will be provided. Schedule 5, part 1 repeals the legislative basis of the following: children's services plan, behaviour support plan, class size reduction plan, education development plan, school organisation plan, early years development and childcare plan, and the adoption services plan.

plain guide to the Children Act 2004

(2) Regulations under this section may in particular make provision as to-
   (a) the matters to be dealt with in a plan under this section;
   (b) the period to which a plan under this section is to relate;
   (c) when and how a plan under this section must be published;
   (d) keeping a plan under this section under review;
   (e) consultation to be carried out before a plan under this section is published;
   (f) implementation of a plan under this section.

Regulations can prescribe the content, timescale, publication and review of the CYPP, the consultation required during the plan's preparation and the implementation plan.

(3) The matters for which provision may be made under subsection (2)(a) include in particular-
   (a) the arrangements made or to be made under section 25 by a children's services authority in Wales;
   (b) the strategy or proposals in relation to children and relevant young persons of any person or body with whom a children's services authority in Wales makes or proposes to make such arrangements.

The regulations may require the cooperation arrangements made under s. 25 to be included in the plan and the strategic plans for children of other bodies.

(4) Regulations under this section may require a children's services authority in Wales to obtain the Assembly's approval before publishing a plan under this section; and may provide that the Assembly may modify a plan before approving it.

Regulations may require a CSA to seek approval of the plan from the Assembly, and the Assembly can give itself power by regulations to modify a plan.

(5) A children's services authority in Wales must have regard to any guidance given to them by the Assembly in relation to how they are to discharge their functions under regulations under this section.

A CSA must have regard to guidance on the discharge of this planning function. The Explanatory Notes state that guidance will support greater coherence as to the precise obligation of CSAs and their partners and to give a statutory basis to the Children and Young People's Framework Partnerships and Children's Partnerships that are already in existence. The plans will rationalise their relationship with the Young People's Partnerships that already have a statutory basis under s.123 of the Learning and Skills Act 2000.

(6) In this section "relevant young persons" means the persons, in addition to children, in relation to whom arrangements under section 25 may be made.

27 Responsibility for functions under sections 25 and 26

(1) A children's services authority in Wales must–
   (a) appoint an officer, to be known as the "lead director for children and young people's services", for the purposes of co-ordinating and overseeing arrangements made under sections 25 and 26; and
   (b) designate one of their members, to be known as the "lead member for children and young people's services", to have as his special care the discharge of the authority's functions under those sections.

(2) A Local Health Board must-
   (a) appoint an officer, to be known as the Board's "lead officer for children and young people's services", for the purposes of the Board's functions under section 25; and
   (b) designate one of the Board's members who is not an officer as its "lead member for children and young people's services" to have the discharge of those functions as his special care.

(3) An NHS trust to which section 25 applies must-
   (a) appoint an executive director, to be known as the trust's "lead executive director for children and young people's services", for the purposes of the trust's functions under that section; and

---

The Children and Young People's Plan covers the same group of young people as the duty to cooperate specifies in s. 25(10).

Each CSA in Wales must appoint a 'lead officer' for the purpose of overseeing and coordinating services for children and young people. A 'lead member' must be appointed to have 'special care' for the discharge of the authority's functions for children and young people. Note: by virtue of paragraph 2 of schedule 2, local authorities in Wales will retain both a Chief Education Officer and a Director of Social Services and the 'lead officer' role will not affect their existing service delivery responsibilities. The Explanatory Note states that 'the lead director will ensure that the partnership planning process is given a high profile within the local authority and acts as a driver for strategic planning for children and young people in the local authority area.'

Each local health board in Wales must appoint a 'lead officer' and 'lead member' for children and young people's services.

Each NHS trust in Wales must appoint a 'lead executive director' and 'lead non-executive director' for children and young peoples' services.

(b) designate one of the trust's non-executive directors as its "lead nonexecutive director for children and young people's services" to have the discharge of those functions as his special care.

(4) Each children's services authority in Wales, Local Health Board and NHS trust to which section 25 applies must have regard to any guidance given to them by the Assembly in relation to-
(a) their functions under this section;
(b) the responsibilities of the persons appointed or designated by them under this section.

Local authorities and the NHS bodies named in this section must have regard to any guidance issued by the Assembly.

28 Arrangements to safeguard and promote welfare: Wales

(1) This section applies to each of the following-
(a) a children's services authority in Wales;
(b) a Local Health Board;
(c) an NHS trust all or most of whose hospitals, establishments and facilities are situated in Wales;
(d) the police authority and chief officer of police for a police area in Wales;
(e) the British Transport Police Authority, so far as exercising functions in relation to Wales;
(f) a local probation board for an area in Wales;
(g) a youth offending team for an area in Wales;
(h) the governor of a prison or secure training centre in Wales (or, in the case of a contracted out prison or secure training centre, its director);
(i) any person to the extent that he is providing services pursuant to arrangements made by a children's services authority in Wales under section 123(1)(b) of the Learning and Skills Act 2000 (c. 21) (youth support services).

The duty to safeguard and promote the welfare of all children is given to a wide range of bodies. Section 175 of the Education Act 2002 gives a similar duty to LEAs and the governing bodies of maintained schools and further education colleges. Local authorities, as a social services function, have long had a general duty to safeguard and promote the welfare of children within their area who are in need and a specific duty in respect of looked-after children (ss 17 and 22 of Children Act 1989). The list is similar to the 'relevant partners' of s. 25 with the addition of the British Transport Police, prisons and secure training establishments. Where a local authority secures the youth support service from an external body, that body comes within the scope of s. 28 also.

(2) Each person and body to whom this section applies must make arrangements for ensuring that-
(a) their functions are discharged having regard to the need to safeguard and promote the welfare of children; and
(b) any services provided by another person pursuant to arrangements made by the person or body in

Each body mentioned in subsection (1) must carry out its functions having regard to the need to safeguard and promote the welfare of children. Paragraph (b) makes clear that the duty extends to contracted services that cover services where privatised and also services that

the discharge of their functions are provided having regard to that need.

(3) In the case of a children's services authority in Wales, the reference in subsection (2) to functions of the authority does not include functions to which section 175 of the Education Act 2002 (c. 32) applies.

have historically been contracted, such as the general practitioner service.

Section 175 of the 2002 Act already places a duty on the LEA to safeguard and promote the welfare of children and have regard to guidance. The LEA, as a local authority, is also the CSA as defined by s. 65(1). This subsection means that the s. 175 duty applies to a CSA's education functions and the s.28 duty (of the Children Act 2004) applies to non-education functions.

(4) The persons and bodies referred to in subsection (1)(a) to (c) and (i) must in discharging their duty under this section have regard to any guidance given to them for the purpose by the Assembly.

Those bodies for whom the Assembly is responsible must have regard to any guidance issued by the Assembly.

(5) The persons and bodies referred to in subsection (1)(d) to (h) must in discharging their duty under this section have regard to any guidance given to them for the purpose by the Secretary of State after consultation with the Assembly.

The bodies for whom the Secretary of State is responsible (police and youth justice bodies) must have regard to guidance issued by the Secretary of State after consultation with the Assembly.

29 Information databases: Wales

(1) The Assembly may for the purpose of arrangements under section 25 or 28 above or under section 175 of the Education Act 2002-
  (a) by regulations require children's services authorities in Wales to establish and operate databases containing information in respect of persons to whom such arrangements relate;
  (b) itself establish and operate, or make arrangements for the operation and establishment of, one or more databases containing such information.

Regulations, which require the consent of the Secretary of State, can require CSAs to establish and operate information databases 'in respect of persons'. Alternatively, the Assembly may establish, or make arrangements for another body to establish, one or more databases containing information. See comment on s. 12

However, the databases and their use must be to help the CSA, relevant partners and other bodies carry out their duties to cooperate, and safeguard and promote the welfare of children, under ss. 25 or

(2) The Assembly may for the purposes of arrangements under subsection (1)(b) by regulations establish a body corporate to establish and operate one or more databases.

28 of the Children Act 2004 or s. 175 of the Education Act 2002.

If the Assembly decides to ask another body to operate the databases, regulations must establish a corporate body to carry out the task, i.e. this effectively limits the body to the public sector.

(3) A database under this section may only include information falling within subsection (4) in relation to a person to whom arrangements specified in subsection (1) relate.

A child's details can only be placed on a database if a body with a duty to safeguard and promote the welfare of children holds the information. In practice, this will include virtually all children, as local health boards will hold information on live births. Children not born in Wales can be recorded when seeking services, e.g. education and primary health care.

(4) The information referred to in subsection (3) is information of the following descriptions in relation to a person-
  (a) his name, address, gender and date of birth;
  (b) a number identifying him;
  (c) the name and contact details of any person with parental responsibility for him (within the meaning of section 3 of the Children Act 1989 (c. 41)) or who has care of him at any time;
  (d) details of any education being received by him (including the name and contact details of any educational institution attended by him);
  (e) the name and contact details of any person providing primary medical services in relation to him under Part 1 of the National Health Service Act 1977 (c. 49);
  (f) the name and contact details of any person providing to him services of such description as the Assembly may by regulations specify;
  (g) information as to the existence of any cause for concern in relation to him;
  (h) information of such other description, not including medical records or other personal records, as the Assembly may by regulations specify.

The information that the database can contain is found in this subsection and includes basic identifying information (name, gender, date of birth), a unique number, parental information, the provision of the basic universal services of education and primary health care, the provision of specialist services to be defined in regulations, and whether a practitioner has a cause for concern about the child. Other information can be added by regulations but paragraph (h) excludes the inclusion of case notes and case histories.

(5) The Assembly may by regulations make provision in relation to the establishment and operation of any database or databases under this section.

The Assembly may by regulations provide for the establishment, management and operation of any database or databases.

(6) Regulations under subsection (5) may in particular make provision-
   (a) as to the information which must or may be contained in any database under this section (subject to subsection (3));
   (b) requiring a person or body specified in subsection (7) to disclose information for inclusion in the database;
   (c) permitting a person or body specified in subsection (8) to disclose information for inclusion in the database;
   (d) permitting or requiring the disclosure of information included in any such database;
   (e) permitting or requiring any person to be given access to any such database for the purpose of adding or reading information;
   (f) as to the conditions on which such access must or may be given;
   (g) as to the length of time for which information must or may be retained;
   (h) as to procedures for ensuring the accuracy of information included in any such database;
   (i) in a case where a database is established by virtue of subsection (1)(b), requiring children's services authorities in Wales to participate in the operation of the database.

A list of issues that might be covered in the regulations made under subsection (5) includes requiring or permitting specified persons or bodies to disclose information to the database, requiring or permitting any person to be given access to the database for adding or retrieving information, the length of time that information can be included on a database and procedures for checking the accuracy of information on a database. Should the Assembly decide to establish a national database or databases, CSAs can be required to participate in the operation of such databases.

(7) The persons and bodies referred to in subsection (6)(b) are-
   (a) the persons and bodies specified in section 28(1);
   (b) the National Council for Education and Training for Wales;
   (c) the governing body of a maintained school in Wales (within the meaning of section 175 of the Education Act 2002 (c. 32));
   (d) the governing body of an institution in Wales within the further education sector (within the meaning of that section);
   (e) the proprietor of an independent school in Wales (within the meaning of the Education Act 1996 (c. 56));
   (f) a person or body of such other description as the Assembly may by regulations specify.

Lists bodies that can be required to disclose information to a database. These are both providers of universal services (the CSAs, youth support service, police and NHS bodies) and the further education provided by ELWa, maintained school governing bodies, further education colleges and proprietors of independent schools.

(8) The persons and bodies referred to in subsection (6)(c) are-
  (a) a person registered in Wales for child minding or the provision of day care under Part 10A of the Children Act 1989 (c. 41);
  (b) a voluntary organisation exercising functions or engaged in activities in relation to persons to whom arrangements specified in subsection (1) relate;
  (c) the Commissioners of Inland Revenue;
  (d) a registered social landlord;
  (e) a person or body of such other description as the Assembly may by regulations specify.

Lists bodies that are permitted to disclose information to a database, including childminders and day-care providers, voluntary organisations, Inland Revenue and registered social landlords.

(9) The Assembly and the Secretary of State may provide information for inclusion in a database under this section.

The Assembly and UK government departments may supply information, for example benefit records from the DWP.

(10) The provision which may be made under subsection (6)(e) includes provision for a person of a description specified in the regulations to determine what must or may be done under the regulations.

Regulations may allow for the delegation of decisions about whether to give a person access to the database to the person or body (Assembly, corporate body or CSA) who established it.

(11) Regulations under subsection (5) may also provide that anything which may be done under regulations under subsection (6)(c) to (e) or (9) may be done notwithstanding any rule of common law which prohibits or restricts the disclosure of information.

Allows common law requirements on the disclosure of information to be overridden by permitted persons or bodies providing or accessing information to a database.

(12) Regulations under subsections (1)(a) and (5) may only be made with the consent of the Secretary of State.

Requires the consent of the Secretary of State before the Assembly can make regulations under this section.

(13) Any person or body establishing or operating a database under this section must in the establishment or operation of the database have regard to any guidance, and comply with any direction, given to that person by the Assembly.

Database operators must comply with any direction of the Assembly over the operation of a database and have must regard to statutory guidance.

(14) Guidance or directions under subsection (13) may in particular relate to-
  (a) the management of a database under this section;
  (b) the technical specifications for any such database;
  (c) the security of any such database;

Lists matters that can be the subject of a direction or guidance under subsection (12), clearly indicating that directions must be related to technical, security and operational

(d) the transfer and comparison of information between databases under this section;

(e) the giving of advice in relation to rights under the Data Protection Act 1998 (c. 29).

30 Inspection of functions under this Part

(1) Chapter 6 of Part 2 of the Health and Social Care (Community Health and Standards) Act 2003 (c. 43) (functions of the Assembly in relation to social services) shall apply as if anything done by a children's services authority in Wales in the exercise of functions to which this section applies were a Welsh local authority social service within the meaning of that Part.

(2) This section applies to the following functions of a children's services authority-
(a) the authority's functions under section 25 or 26, except so far as relating to education, training or youth support services (within the meaning of section 123 of the Learning and Skills Act 2000 (c. 21));
(b) the authority's functions under section 28;
(c) any function conferred on the authority under section 29.

Local Safeguarding Children Boards

31 Establishment of LSCBs in Wales

(1) Each children's services authority in Wales must establish a Local Safeguarding Children Board for their area.

Sidebar notes:

issues including subject rights under the Data Protection Act 1998.

Enables the Assembly probably through the Social Services Inspectorate for Wales to inspect the CSA functions specified in subsection (2).

The functions are the cooperation and planning duties (except where Estyn already has a role), safeguarding duties and information sharing roles.

The Act requires each CSA to establish a LSCB. The LSCB is a statutory body which is charged with ensuring the effectiveness of local arrangements and services to safeguard children, including services provided by individual agencies. It will be the main mechanism by which the CSA can make the other partners accountable for the provision of services to children. The Boards will replace the non-statutory ACPCs.

Each CSA must set up a LSCB, but see subsection (9).

(2) A Board established under this section must include such representative or representatives of-
   (a) the authority by which it is established, and
   (b) each Board partner of that authority, as the Assembly may by regulations prescribe.

Regulations will prescribe that the authority and each partner (see subsection (3)) must be represented on the LSCB. The wording allows a body to be represented by more than one representative or a representative could represent more than one body, as provided by regulations.

(3) For the purposes of this section each of the following is a Board partner of a children's services authority in Wales-
   (a) the chief officer of police for a police area any part of which falls within the area of the authority;
   (b) a local probation board for an area any part of which falls within the area of the authority;
   (c) a youth offending team for an area any part of which falls within the area of the authority;
   (d) a Local Health Board for an area any part of which falls within the area of the authority;
   (e) an NHS trust providing services in the area of the authority;
   (f) the governor of any secure training centre within the area of the authority (or, in the case of a contracted out secure training centre, its director);
   (g) the governor of any prison in the area of the authority which ordinarily detains children (or, in the case of a contracted out prison, its director).

The bodies that must be represented on the LSCB are:
- *CSA*
- *police force*
- *probation service*
- *youth offending team*
- *Local Health Board and NHS trusts providing services in the area*
- *Youth Support Service*
- *secure training centres*
- *prisons that ordinarily detain children.*

(4) Regulations under subsection (2) that make provision in relation to a Board partner referred to in subsection (3)(a) to (c), (f) or (g) may only be made with the consent of the Secretary of State.

Regulations under subsection 2 that affect the police or youth justice services require the permission of the Secretary of State.

(5) A children's services authority in Wales must take reasonable steps to ensure that the Local Safeguarding Children Board established by them includes representatives of relevant persons and bodies of such descriptions as may be prescribed by the Assembly in regulations.

In addition to the membership prescribed by subsection (3), the Assembly may prescribe in regulations other relevant persons and bodies that the CSA must take reasonable steps to ensure are representative members of the LSCB, e.g. schools and voluntary groups.

(6) A Local Safeguarding Children Board established under this section may also include representatives of such other relevant persons or bodies as the authority

A CSA, after consulting the LSCB, can add representatives of other relevant persons or bodies to the Board.

by which it is established consider, after consulting their Board partners, should be represented on it.

(7) For the purposes of subsections (5) and (6), relevant persons and bodies are persons and bodies of any nature exercising functions or engaged in activities relating to children in the area of the authority in question.

Representatives added to the Board by virtue of subsections (4) and (5) must be 'engaged in activities' with children in the area.

(8) In the establishment and operation of a Local Safeguarding Children Board under this section-
 (a) the authority establishing it must co-operate with each of their Board partners; and
 (b) each Board partner must co-operate with the authority.

The CSA and the partners must cooperate in the establishment of the LSCB.

(9) Two or more children's services authorities in Wales may discharge their respective duties under subsection (1) by establishing a Local Safeguarding Children Board for their combined area (and where they do so, any reference in this section and sections 32 to 34 to the authority establishing the Board shall be read as a reference to the authorities establishing it).

Two or more CSAs may establish a joint LSCB, although this seems an unlikely option for virtually all CSAs.

32 Functions and procedure of LSCBs in Wales

(1) The objective of a Local Safeguarding Children Board established under section 31 is-
 (a) to co-ordinate what is done by each person or body represented on the Board for the purposes of safeguarding and promoting the welfare of children in the area of the authority by which it is established; and
 (b) to ensure the effectiveness of what is done by each such person or body for those purposes.

An LSCB must coordinate, and ensure the effectiveness of, the work of each body or person represented on the Board in safeguarding and promoting the welfare of children.

(2) A Local Safeguarding Children Board established under section 31 is to have such functions in relation to its objective as the Assembly may by regulations prescribe (which may in particular include functions of review or investigation).

The Assembly may prescribe by regulations the functions of the LSCB, which will be largely based on the functions of the ACPC, as set out in Working Together to Safeguard Children (DoH, HO, DfEE, 1999).

(3) The Assembly may by regulations make provision as to the procedures to be followed by a Local

The Assembly may prescribe by regulations the procedures of the

Safeguarding Children Board established under section 31.

LSCB, for example the keeping of a register of attendance.

33 Funding of LSCBs in Wales

(1) Any person or body specified in subsection (3) may make payments towards expenditure incurred by, or for purposes connected with, a Local Safeguarding Children Board established under section 31-
  (a) by making the payments directly, or
  (b) by contributing to a fund out of which the payments may be made.

LSCBs are funded by direct payments or by pooling funds from contributors.

(2) Any person or body specified in subsection (3) may provide staff, goods, services, accommodation or other resources for purposes connected with a Local Safeguarding Children Board established under section 31.

Contributions may be in kind, in the form of staff, accommodation, etc.

(3) The persons and bodies referred to in subsections (1) and (2) are-
  (a) the children's services authority in Wales by which the Board is established;
  (b) any person who is a Board partner of the authority under section 31(3)(a) to (e);
  (c) in a case where the governor of a secure training centre or prison is a Board partner of the authority, the Secretary of State; and
  (d) in a case where the director of a contracted out secure training centre or prison is a Board partner of the authority, the contractor.

The contributors to the running costs are the CSA and Board partners. In the case of the governor of a secure training centre or prison, the Secretary of State is the contributor, although if the service has been contracted out, the contractor is the contributor.

34 LSCBs in Wales: supplementary

(1) The Assembly may by regulations make provision as to the functions of children's services authorities in Wales relating to Local Safeguarding Children Boards established by them.

The Assembly may prescribe by regulations the administrative and support services that CSAs must provide to LSCBs.

(2) A children's services authority in Wales and each of their Board partners must, in exercising their functions relating to a Local Safeguarding Children Board, have regard to any guidance given to them for the purpose by the Assembly.

This Assembly can issue statutory guidance to the CSA and Board partners about the operation of the LSCB, for example the funding and arrangements for investigating a child death.

(3) The Assembly must obtain the consent of the Secretary of State before giving guidance under subsection (2) at any time after the coming into force of any of paragraphs (a) to (c), (f) or (g) of section 31(3).º

Guidance requires the consent of the Secretary of State once membership of the LSCB by the police and youth justice bodies comes into force.

Part 4   Advisory and support services for family proceedings

This Part provides for the devolution of CAFCASS functions in Wales to the Assembly.

CAFCASS was established on 1 April 2001 by the Criminal Justice and Court Services Act 2000 as a new non-departmental public body for England and Wales. CAFCASS brought together the functions of three services, which supported vulnerable children in family proceedings: the local authority Family Court Welfare Service, the work of the Guardians ad Litem and Reporting Officers and the Children's Division of the Official Solicitor.

The primary duties of CAFCASS, in respect of family proceedings in which the welfare of children is or may be in question, as set out in the 2000 Act, are to:
- safeguard and promote the welfare of the child
- give advice to any court about any application made to it in such proceedings
- make provision for children to be represented in such proceedings
- provide information, advice and other support for children and their families.

Responsibility for CAFCASS transferred to the DfES from the Department of Constitutional Affairs on 12 January 2004. Consistent with this change, responsibility for the service in Wales is being transferred to the National Assembly for Wales. Part 4 of the Children Act 2004 contains the necessary legislation.

CAFCASS functions in Wales

35 Functions of the Assembly relating to family proceedings

(1) In respect of family proceedings in which the welfare of children ordinarily resident in Wales is or may be in question, it is a function of the Assembly to - (a) safeguard and promote the welfare of the children;
   (b) give advice to any court about any application made to it in such proceedings;
   (c) make provision for the children to be represented in such proceedings;
   (d) provide information, advice and other support for the children and their families.

The CAFCASS functions found in s.12(1) of the Criminal Justice and Court Services Act 2000 in respect of children ordinarily resident in Wales are transferred to the National Assembly for Wales. A CAFCASS for Wales is not created.

(2) The Assembly must also make provision for the performance of the functions conferred on Welsh family proceedings officers by virtue of any enactment (whether or not they are exercisable for the purposes of subsection (1)).

The Assembly will carry out its new responsibility through 'Welsh family proceedings officers' (see subsection (4) and s.35). This subsection requires the Assembly to ensure that these officers fulfil the requirements laid on them by statute.

plain guide to the Children Act 2004

(3) In subsection (1), "family proceedings" has the meaning given by section 12 of the Criminal Justice and Court Services Act 2000 (c. 43).

> See s.12(5) of the 2000 Act for the definition of 'family proceedings', which in turn relies on the Matrimonial and Family Proceedings Act 1984. Family proceedings cover family maintenance following break up of parental relationship, paternity disputes, residence disputes, contact disputes and care proceedings and are normally heard in private in Magistrates' Courts.

(4) In this Part, "Welsh family proceedings officer" means -
 (a) any member of the staff of the Assembly appointed to exercise the functions of a Welsh family proceedings officer; and
 (b) any other individual exercising functions of a Welsh family proceedings officer by virtue of section 36(2) or (4).

> Defines a 'Welsh family proceedings officer' as a member of staff of the Assembly appointed to carry out the functions of a Welsh family proceedings officer or someone appointed by another organisation that is contracted to the Assembly to perform the Assembly's functions as defined in subsection (1).

36 Ancillary powers of the Assembly

(1) The Assembly may make arrangements with organisations under which the organisations perform the functions of the Assembly under section 35 on its behalf.

> The Assembly can make arrangements with other organisations to perform its CAFCASS functions, which includes the option of contracting out those functions.

(2) Arrangements under subsection (1) may provide for the organisations to designate individuals who may perform functions of Welsh family proceedings officers.

> Any such organisation appointed under subsection (1) can designate individuals to perform the functions of 'Welsh family proceedings officers'.

(3) The Assembly may only make an arrangement under subsection (1) if it is of the opinion-
 (a) that the functions in question will be performed efficiently and to the required standard; and
 (b) that the arrangement represents good value for money.

> The Assembly can set performance and value for money standards for an organisation performing functions under this section.

(4) The Assembly may make arrangements with individuals under which they may perform functions of Welsh family proceedings officers.

> The Assembly can use, for example, self-employed practitioners to carry out the functions of the Welsh family proceedings officers.

(5) The Assembly may make arrangements with an organisation or individual under which staff of the Assembly engaged in the exercise of its functions under section 35 may work for the organisation or individual.

The Assembly can second staff to organisations carrying out the Assembly's functions under s.35.

(6) The Assembly may make arrangements with an organisation or individual under which any services provided by the Assembly's staff to the Assembly in the exercise of its functions under section 35 are also made available to the organisation or individual.

The Assembly can provide services to organisations and individuals carrying out the Assembly's functions under s.35.

(7) The Assembly may charge for anything done under arrangements under subsection (5) and (6).

The Assembly can charge for the provision of staff or services where functions have been contracted out to individuals or organisations.

(8) In this section, references to organisations include public bodies and private or voluntary organisations.

Organisations providing contracted out services can include public, private and voluntary bodies.

37 Welsh family proceedings officers

(1) The Assembly may authorise a Welsh family proceedings officer of a description prescribed in regulations made by the Secretary of State-
   (a) to conduct litigation in relation to any proceedings in any court,
   (b) to exercise a right of audience in any proceedings in any court, in the exercise of his functions.

See s.15(1) of the 2000 Act. A 'Welsh family proceedings officer' may conduct litigation or exercise a right of audience, subject to any regulations made by the Secretary of State (because these are 'non-devolved' matters).

(2) A Welsh family proceedings officer exercising a right to conduct litigation by virtue of subsection (1)(a) who would otherwise have such a right by virtue of section 28(2)(a) of the Courts and Legal Services Act 1990 (c. 41) is to be treated as having acquired that right solely by virtue of this section.

See s.15(2) of the 2000 Act. The right to conduct litigation in subsection (1) is defined as coming from subsection (1) and not from any qualification that person might have.

(3) A Welsh family proceedings officer exercising a right of audience by virtue of subsection (1)(b) who would otherwise have such a right by virtue of section 27(2)(a) of the Courts and Legal Services Act 1990 is to be treated as having acquired that right solely by virtue of this section.

See s.15(3) of the 2000 Act. The right to exercise an audience in subsection (1) is defined as coming from subsection (1) and not from any qualification that person might have.

(4) A Welsh family proceedings officer may, subject to rules of court, be cross-examined in any proceedings to the same extent as any witness.

See s.16(1) of the 2000 Act. A Welsh family proceedings officer may be cross examined in any

(5) But a Welsh family proceedings officer may not be cross-examined merely because he is exercising a right to conduct litigation or a right of audience granted in accordance with this section.

court proceedings i.e. be treated as any other witness.

See s.16(2) of the 2000 Act. Subsection (4) only applies to the evidence that the Welsh family proceedings officer is submitting not because the Welsh family proceedings officer has a right of audience.

(6) In this section, "right to conduct litigation" and "right of audience" have the same meanings as in section 119 of the Courts and Legal Services Act 1990.

See s.15(4) of the 2000 Act.

38 Inspections

(1) Her Majesty's Inspectorate of Court Administration must at the request of the Assembly inspect, and report to the Assembly on-
  (a) the discharge by the Assembly of its functions under this Part; and
  (b) the discharge by Welsh family proceedings officers of their functions under this Part and any other enactment.

See s.17 of the 2000 Act. The Assembly can seek an inspection of how well it has exercised its advisory and support services functions for children in family proceedings from Her Majesty's Inspectorate of Court Administration. The inspection can also cover the work of Welsh family proceedings officers.

(2) The Assembly may only make a request under subsection (1) with the consent of the Secretary of State.

Any request under subsection (1) requires the consent of the Secretary of State as court administration is a 'non-devloved' matter.

39 Protection of children

(1) The Protection of Children Act 1999 (c. 14) ("the 1999 Act") shall have effect as if the Assembly, in performing its functions under sections 35 and 36, were a child care organisation within the meaning of that Act.

The Protection of Children Act 1999 is applied to the Assembly by treating it as a childcare organisation for its work on providing advisory and support services for children in family proceedings.

(2) Arrangements which the Assembly makes with an organisation under section 36(1) must provide that, before selecting an individual to be employed under the arrangements in a child care position, the organisation-
  (a) must ascertain whether the individual is included in any of the lists mentioned in section 7(1) of the 1999 Act, and
  (b) if he is included in any of those lists, must not select him for that employment.

The Assembly is required to check on the suitability of any individual engaged to do work under this part of the Act.

(3) Such arrangements must provide that, if at any time the organisation has power to refer an individual who is or has been employed in a child care position under the arrangements to the Secretary of State under section 2 of the 1999 Act (inclusion in list on reference following disciplinary actions etc), the organisation must so refer him.

The Assembly is required to report any individual who may need to be disqualified from working under this Part.

(4) In this section, "child care position" and "employment" have the same meanings as in the 1999 Act.

'Child care position' is defined.

40 Advisory and support services for family proceedings: supplementary

Schedule 3 (which makes supplementary and consequential provision relating to this Part, including provision relating to functions of Welsh family proceedings officers) has effect.

This section brings Schedule 3 into effect.

41 Sharing of information

(1) The Assembly and the Children and Family Court Advisory and Support Service may provide any information to each other for the purposes of their respective functions under this Part and Part 1 of the Criminal Justice and Court Services Act 2000 (c. 43).

Enables the Assembly and CAFCASS to share information where it is in the interests of children and good management.

(2) A Welsh family proceedings officer and an officer of the Service (within the meaning given by section 11(3) of that Act) may provide any information to each other for the purposes of any of their respective functions.

Enables the Welsh family proceedings officers and CAFCASS officers to share information.

Transfers

42 Transfer of property from CAFCASS to Assembly

(1) For the purposes of the exercise of functions conferred on the Assembly by or under this Part, the Assembly and the Secretary of State may jointly by order make one or more schemes for the transfer to the Assembly of property, rights and liabilities of the Children and Family Court Advisory and Support Service (in this section, "CAFCASS").

The Assembly and Secretary of State may, by order, transfer property from CAFCASS to the Assembly.

(2) The reference in subsection (1) to rights and liabilities does not include rights and liabilities under a contract of employment.

Excludes employment rights.

(3) A scheme under this section may-
   (a) specify the property, rights and liabilities to be transferred by the scheme; or
   (b) provide for the determination, in accordance with the scheme, of the property, rights and liabilities to be transferred by the scheme.

The scheme transferring property must specify the property, or a means of determining the property, to be transferred.

(4) A scheme under this section may include provision for the creation of rights, or the imposition of liabilities, in relation to property transferred by the scheme.

Rights and liabilities on transferred properties can be created by the transfer.

(5) A scheme under this section has effect in relation to any property, rights and liabilities to which it applies despite any provision (of whatever nature) which would otherwise prevent, penalise or restrict their transfer.

The transfer scheme can override other provisions that restrict the transfer.

(6) A right of pre-emption or reverter or other similar right does not operate or become exercisable as a result of any transfer under a scheme under this section; and in the case of such a transfer, any such right has effect as if the Assembly were the same person in law as CAFCASS and as if the transfer had not taken place.

A reverter on any property does not take effect solely because the property is transferred.

(7) The Assembly is to pay such compensation as is just to any person in respect of any right which would, apart from subsections (5) and (6), have operated in favour of, or become exercisable by, that person but which, in consequence of the operation of those subsections, cannot subsequently operate in his favour or become exercisable by him.

The Assembly is required to pay compensation in certain cases.

(8) A scheme under this section may provide for the determination of any disputes as to whether and, if so, how much compensation is payable under subsection (7).

The scheme may provide for the settling of disputes.

(9) Subsections (5) to (8) apply in relation to the creation of rights in relation to property as they apply in relation to a transfer of property.

This is a technical subsection.

(10) A certificate issued by the Secretary of State and the Assembly jointly that any property, rights or liabilities have or have not been transferred by a scheme under this section is conclusive evidence as to whether they have or have not been so transferred.

This is a technical subsection.

43 Transfer of staff from CAFCASS to Assembly

(1) For the purpose of the exercise of functions conferred on the Assembly by or under this Part, the Assembly and the Secretary of State may jointly by order make one or more schemes for the transfer of employees of CAFCASS to the Assembly.

| The Assembly and Secretary of State may by order transfer employees from CAFCASS to the Assembly.

(2) A scheme under this section may apply-
   (a) to any description of employees of CAFCASS;
   (b) to any individual employee of CAFCASS.

| The transfer scheme may refer to individual employees or groups of employees.

(3) A contract of employment of an employee transferred under a scheme under this section-
   (a) is not terminated by the transfer; and
   (b) has effect from the date of the transfer under the scheme as if originally made between the employee and the Assembly.

| Provides for continuity of employment on transfer.

(4) Where an employee is so transferred-
   (a) all the rights, powers, duties and liabilities of CAFCASS under or in connection with the contract of employment are by virtue of this subsection transferred to the Assembly on the date of the transfer under the scheme; and
   (b) anything done before that date by or in relation to CAFCASS in respect of that contract or the employee is to be treated from that date as having been done by or in relation to the Assembly. This subsection does not prejudice the generality of subsection (3).

| Provides for CAFCASS employment responsibilities to transfer to the Assembly.

(5) But if the employee informs the Assembly or CAFCASS that he objects to the transfer-
   (a) subsections (3) and (4) do not apply; and
   (b) his contract of employment is terminated immediately before the date of transfer but the employee is not to be treated, for any reason, as having been dismissed by CAFCASS.

| Technical employment provisions.

(6) This section does not prejudice any right of an employee to terminate his contract of employment if (apart from the change of employer) a substantial change is made to his detriment in his working conditions.

| Technical employment provisions.

(7) A scheme may be made under this section only if any requirements about consultation prescribed in regulations made by the Secretary of State and the Assembly jointly have been complied with in relation to each of the employees of CAFCASS to be transferred under the scheme.

Technical employment provisions.

(8) In this section "CAFCASS" has the same meaning as in section 41.

Defines CAFCASS for this section.

Part 5   Miscellaneous

A number of further provisions with regard to private fostering, childminding and day care, local authority services and other provisions.

Private fostering

A privately fostered child is defined under s.66 of the Children Act 1989 as a child who is under the age of 16 (18 if disabled) and cared for by someone other than a parent, person with parental responsibility or close relative. A child is not privately fostered if the arrangement is for fewer than 28 days. Schedule 8 of the 1989 Act requires private foster parents to inform the LA that they are fostering. Criticisms of the law on private fostering were made in the Climbie Inquiry (UK.Parliament.HoC, 2003, p.350). Arguably, Victoria was privately fostered. This Act presents two different changes to the law. The Government is planning for the early introduction of s.44, which enables greater supervision by LAs of private foster carers. Section 45 (England) and 46 (Wales) provide a more rigorous system of registration and monitoring of private foster carers, which may be introduced if the changes introduced in s.44 are deemed to be insufficient. Section 47 is a 'sunset' clause, which requires the more rigorous scheme to be introduced within four years or not at all.

44 Amendments to notification scheme

It is expected this section will commence on July 2005.

(1) Section 67 of the Children Act 1989 (c. 41) (welfare of privately fostered children) is amended as specified in subsections (2) to (6).

Amendments are made to s.67 of the Children Act 1989, which pro-

plain guide to the Children Act 2004

(2) In subsection (1)-
   (a) after "who are" insert "or are proposed to be";
   (b) after "is being" insert "or will be";
   (c) for "caring for" substitute "concerned with".

The scope of s.67 is enlarged to include children who are proposed to be fostered privately.

(3) After subsection (2) insert-
   "(2A) Regulations under subsection (2)(b) may impose requirements as to the action to be taken by a local authority for the purposes of discharging their duty under subsection (1) where they have received notification of a proposal that a child be privately fostered."

Enables regulations to be made about what the local authority must do when notified about a proposed private fostering arrangement.

(4) In subsection (3) for "to visit privately fostered children" substitute "for the purpose".

Local authority officers to be authorised to work generally on the welfare of privately-fostered children, not just to visit such children.

(5) In subsection (5)-
   (a) after "child who is" insert "or is proposed to be";
   (b) after "is being" insert "or will be".

This is a consequential amendment.

(6) After subsection (5) insert-
   "(6) The Secretary of State may make regulations requiring a local authority to monitor the way in which the authority discharge their functions under this Part (and the regulations may in particular require the authority to appoint an officer for that purpose)."

Regulations may be made that require local authorities to monitor their work with privately-fostered children.

(7) In Schedule 8 to that Act (privately fostered children) after paragraph 7 insert-
   "7A Every local authority must promote public awareness in their area of requirements as to notification for which provision is made under paragraph 7."

Local authorities must provide local information about the need for private foster carers to register with the local authority.

(8) The reference to that Act in Schedule 1 to the National Assembly for Wales (Transfer of Functions) Order 1999 (S.I. 1999/672) is to be treated as referring to that Act as amended by this section.

Applies this section to Wales.

45 Power to establish registration scheme in England

(1) The Secretary of State may by regulations require any person who fosters a child privately in the area of a children's services authority in England to be registered for private fostering by that authority in accordance with the regulations.

Regulations may require all private foster carers to register with the CSA.

(2) Regulations under this section may make supplementary provision relating to the registration of persons for private fostering, including provision as to-
   (a) how a person applies for registration and the procedure to be followed in considering an application;
   (b) the requirements to be satisfied before a person may be registered;
   (c) the circumstances in which a person is disqualified from being registered;
   (d) the circumstances in which an application for registration may or must be granted or refused;
   (e) the payment of a fee on the making or granting of an application for registration;
   (f) the imposition of conditions on registration and the variation or cancellation of such conditions;
   (g) the circumstances in which a person's registration may be, or be regarded as, cancelled;
   (h) the making of appeals against any determination of a children's services authority in England in relation to a person's registration;
   (i) temporary registration, or circumstances in which a person may be regarded as registered;
   (j) requirements to be complied with by a children's services authority in England or a person registered under the regulations.

The regulations may specify how the local authority accepts, considers and disposes of applications by persons to foster children privately. A registration fee may be payable. Subsections (3) to (14) make supplementary provisions about the regulations.

(3) The provision which may be made under subsection (2)(a) includes provision that any person who, in an application for registration under the regulations, knowingly makes a statement which is false or misleading in a material particular is guilty of an offence and liable on summary conviction to a fine not exceeding level 5 on the standard scale.

It is an offence to make a false or misleading application.

(4) The requirements for which provision may be made under subsection (2)(b) include requirements relating to-

The CSA must consider both the suitability of the applicant and the suitability of the premises. The latter

(a) the suitability of the applicant to foster children privately;
(b) the suitability of the premises in which it is proposed to foster children privately (including their suitability by reference to any other person living there).

may include the suitability of other persons living on the premises.

(5) The provision which may be made under subsection (2)(c) includes provision that a person may be disqualified where-
(a) an order of a kind specified in the regulations has been made at any time with respect to him;
(b) an order of a kind so specified has been made at any time with respect to any child who has been in his care;
(c) a requirement of a kind so specified has been imposed at any time with respect to any such child, under or by virtue of any enactment;
(d) he has been convicted of a criminal offence of a kind so specified, or a probation order has been made in respect of him for any such offence or he has been discharged absolutely or conditionally for any such offence;
(e) a prohibition has been imposed on him under any specified enactment;
(f) his rights and powers with respect to a child have at any time been vested in a specified authority under a specified enactment;
(g) he lives in the same household as a person who is himself disqualified from being registered or in a household in which such a person is employed.

Sets out in detail the grounds on which a person can be disqualified from being a private foster carer. For example, regulations will allow the local authority to not register a person who is the parent of a child who has been the subject of a care order. Specified criminal convictions can be the grounds for refusing registration.

(6) The provision which may be made under subsection (2)(c) also includes provision for a children's services authority in England to determine whether a person is or is not to be disqualified.

The CSA may determine that a person who is otherwise 'disqualified' can be registered.

(7) The conditions for which provision may be made under subsection (2)(f) include conditions relating to-
(a) the maintenance of premises in which children are, or are proposed to be, privately fostered;
(b) any other persons living at such premises.

Registration conditions may be imposed by the CSA on the maintenance of premises and other persons living at the premises.

(8) The provision which may be made under subsection (2)(j) includes-
(a) a requirement that a person registered under the regulations obtain the consent of the children's

The CSA may require that a registered foster carer seeks consent, from the CSA, to foster a particular child.

services authority in England by whom he is registered before privately fostering a child;
(b) provision relating to the giving of such consent (including provision as to the circumstances in which, or conditions subject to which, it may or must be given).

(9) The provision which may be made under subsection (2)(j) also includes-
(a) a requirement for a children's services authority in England to undertake annual inspections in relation to persons registered under the regulations (whether in fact privately fostering children or not); and
(b) provision for the payment of a fee by registered persons in respect of such inspections.

The CSA may be required to undertake annual inspections of registered foster carers.

(10) Regulations under this section may-
(a) authorise a children's services authority in England to issue a notice to any person whom they believe to be fostering a child privately in their area without being registered in accordance with the regulations; and
(b) provide that a person who, without reasonable excuse, fosters a child privately without being registered in accordance with the regulations while such a notice is issued in respect of him is guilty of an offence and liable on summary conviction to a fine not exceeding level 5 on the standard scale.

It is an offence to continue private fostering once the CSA has issued a notice to an unregistered person who is privately fostering a child.

(11) Regulations under this section may provide that a person registered under the regulations who without reasonable excuse contravenes or otherwise fails to comply with any requirement imposed on him in the regulations is guilty of an offence and liable on summary conviction to a fine not exceeding level 5 on the standard scale.

A registered private foster carer who is in breach of requirements imposed by regulations may be thought to have committed an offence. No offence is created for being in breach of CSA conditions.

(12) Regulations under this section may provide that a person who fosters a child privately while he is disqualified from being registered is guilty of an offence unless-
(a) he is disqualified by virtue of the fact that he lives in the same household as a person who is himself

An offence is committed by a person who privately fosters a child while disqualified.

plain guide to the Children Act 2004

disqualified from being registered or in a household in which such a person is employed; and
(b) he did not know, and had no reasonable grounds for believing, that that person was so disqualified.

(13) Where regulations under this section make provision under subsection (12), they must provide that a person who is guilty of the offence referred to in that subsection is liable on summary conviction to-
(a) a fine not exceeding level 5 on the standard scale, or
(b) a term of imprisonment not exceeding 51 weeks (or, in the case of an offence committed before the commencement of section 281(5) of the Criminal Justice Act 2003 (c. 44), not exceeding six months), or
(c) both.

Provides for the possibility of imprisonment of a person who commits an offence under subsection (12).

(14) Regulations under this section may-
(a) make consequential amendments (including repeals) to sections 67(2) to (6) and 68 to 70 of, and paragraphs 6 to 9 of Schedule 8 to, the Children Act 1989 (c. 41);
(b) amend Schedule 1 to the Local Authority Social Services Act 1970 (c. 42) (social services functions) as to add functions of a children's services authority in England under this section to the functions listed in that Schedule.

Enables consequential changes to be made to the Children Act 1989 and other legislation should the registration scheme be introduced.

(15) Nothing in this section affects the scope of section 64(1).

The usual regulation making powers apply.

(16) For the purposes of this section references to a person fostering a child privately have the same meaning as in the Children Act 1989.

The definition of a person fostering a child privately comes from the Children Act 1989.

46 Power to establish registration scheme in Wales

(1) The Assembly may by regulations require any person who fosters a child privately in the area of a children's services authority in Wales to be registered for private fostering by that authority in accordance with the regulations.

The NAfW may introduce a scheme requiring private foster carers to register for private fostering.

(2) Subsections (2) to (15) of section 44 apply in relation to regulations under this section as they apply in relation to regulations under that section with the substitution for

The NAfW can use the regulation making powers of s.44 (2) to (15) for constructing a scheme in Wales.

references to a children's services authority in England of references to a children's services authority in Wales.

(3) Subsection (16) of that section applies for the purposes of this section.

Applies s.44 (16) to Wales

47 Expiry of powers in sections 45 and 46

(1) If no regulations have been made under section 45 by the relevant time, that section shall (other than for the purposes of section 46(2) and (3)) cease to have effect at that time.

Regulations establishing a registration scheme in England have to be made within the 'relevant time' otherwise the scheme falls.

(2) If no regulations have been made under section 45 by the relevant time, that section shall cease to have effect at that time.

Regulations establishing a registration scheme in Wales have to be made within the 'relevant time' otherwise the scheme falls.

(3) In this section, the relevant time is the end of the period of four years beginning with the day on which this Act is passed.

The end of the 'relevant time' is four years after the Act was passed, that is 15 November 2008.

Child minding and day care

The current law on child minding and day care was recast with the Care Standards Act 2000 amending the Children Act 1989. Responsibility was given to Ofsted to register and inspect child minders and day care in England and to the Assembly in Wales. In the light of experience, amendments were made by the Education Act 2002 and further amendments are made by the Children Act 2004.

48 Child minding and day care

Schedule 4 (which makes provision amending Part 10A of the Children Act 1989 in relation to child minding and day care) has effect.

Adds Schedule 4 to the Act.

Local authority services

Local authority and local education authority legislation is amended covering a range of issues.

49 Payments to foster parents

(1) The appropriate person may by order make provision as to the payments to be made–

The Government received the power to set, by order, the level of

plain guide to the Children Act 2004

(a) by a children's services authority in England or Wales or a person exercising functions on its behalf to a local authority foster parent with whom any child is placed by that authority or person under section 23(2)(a) of the Children Act 1989 (c. 41);

(b) by a voluntary organisation to any person with whom any child is placed by that organisation under section 59(1)(a) of that Act.

payments made by CSAs to foster parents caring for looked after children at the Bill's last Parliamentary stage. The power applies to looked after children placed by local authorities as well as those placed by voluntary organisations. The first use of the order making power in England requires an affirmative resolution of both Houses of Parliament by virtue of s.66(4).

(2) In subsection (1)–
"appropriate person" means–
(a) the Secretary of State, in relation to a children's services authority in England;
(b) the Assembly, in relation to a children's services authority in Wales;
"local authority foster parent" and "voluntary organisation" have the same meanings as in the Children Act 1989 (c. 41).

The order making power is given to the Secretary of State in England and the NAfW in Wales. Other definitions are found in the Children Act 1989.

(3) In section 23(2)(a) of the Children Act 1989 (c. 41), at the end insert "(subject to section 48 of the Children Act 2004)".

The discretion given to local authorities in s.23 (provision of accommodation and maintenance by local authority for children whom they are looking after) of the Children Act 1989 to decide the level of payments to foster parents is made subject to orders made under this section (s.49, Children Act 2004).

(4) In section 59(1)(a) of that Act, at the end insert "(subject to section 48 of the Children Act 2004)".

Similarly, the discretion given to voluntary organisations in s.59 (provision of accommodation by voluntary organisations) of the Children Act 1989 is made subject to orders made under this section.

50 Intervention

(1) Section 497A of the Education Act 1996 (c. 56) (power to secure proper performance of a local education authority's functions) applies in relation to-
(a) the relevant functions of a children's services authority in England, and

Extends the intervention powers of the Secretary of State or NAfW to 'relevant functions' of CSAs in England and Wales. Section 497A (Power to secure proper performance of LEA's functions) is applied

(b) the relevant functions of a children's services authority in Wales, as it applies in relation to the functions of a local education authority referred to in subsection (1) of that section.

to CSAs where a CSA is failing in any respect, in the view of the Secretary of State or NAfW, to perform any relevant function to an adequate standard, or at all.

(2) For the purposes of this section, the relevant functions of a children's services authority in England or Wales are-
(a) functions conferred on or exercisable by the authority which are social services functions, so far as those functions relate to children;
(b) the functions conferred on the authority under sections 23C to 24D of the Children Act 1989 (c. 41) (so far as not falling within paragraph (a)); and
(c) the functions conferred on the authority under sections 10, 12 and 17 above (in the case of a children's services authority in England) or under sections 25, 26 and 29 above (in the case of a children's services authority in Wales).

The 'relevant functions' are:
- social services functions that relate to children
- Children Act 1989 functions relating to children leaving public care
- CSA functions in the Children Act 2004 on co-operation to improve well-being (ss. 10 and 25) and information databases (ss. 12 and 29).

(3) In subsection (2)(a) "social services functions" has the same meaning as in the the Local Authority Social Services Act 1970 (c. 42).

'Social services functions' has the same meaning as in the Local Authority Social Services Act 1970. Schedule 1 specifies provisions in local government and other legislation, which are 'social services functions'.

(4) Sections 497AA and 497B of the Education Act 1996 apply accordingly where powers under section 497A of that Act are exercised in relation to any of the relevant functions of a children's services authority in England or Wales.

Applies ss. 497AA (Power to secure proper performance: duty of authority where directions contemplated) and 497B (Power to secure proper performance: further provisions) to CSAs where intervention is being considered.

(5) In the application of sections 497A(2) to (7), 497AA and 497B of that Act in relation to the relevant functions of a children's services authority in England or Wales, references to the local education authority are to be read as references to the children's services authority in England or Wales.

Makes clear that references to the 'local education authority' should be read as the 'children's services authority' where intervention under this section is being considered.

(6) In subsection (5) of section 497A of that Act, the reference to functions to which that section applies includes (for all purposes) relevant functions of a children's services authority in England or Wales.

Makes clear that the reference to functions in section 497A of the 1996 Act applies to relevant functions of a CSA where intervention is

51 Inspection of local education authorities

In section 38 of the Education Act 1997 (c. 44) (inspection of LEAs), for subsection (2) substitute-
  "(2) An inspection of a local education authority in England under this section shall consist of a review of the way in which the authority are performing any function conferred on them in their capacity as a local education authority, other than a function falling within the remit of the Adult Learning Inspectorate under section 53 of the Learning and Skills Act 2000 (c. 21).
  (2A) An inspection of a local education authority in Wales under this section shall consist of a review of the way in which the authority are performing-
    (a) any function conferred on them in their capacity as a local education authority; and
    (b) the functions conferred on them under sections 25 and 26 so far as relating to education, training or youth support services (within the meaning of section 123 of the Learning and Skills Act 2000 (c. 21))."

being considered under s.50 of the 2004 Act.

Amends s.38 of the Education Act 1997 (Inspection of LEAs) to make it clear that inspections by Ofsted (in England) and Estyn (in Wales) of LEAs can include the performance of any LEA function with the exception, in England, of those functions that are the responsibility of ALI. The reference to ALI is to maintain the current role of this inspectorate (in Wales, Estyn inspects adult learning). The amendment allows, for example, post-16 youth service provision to be inspected under s.38 of the 1997 Act and not as previously under the Learning and Skills Act 2000. Schedule 5, Part 3, makes a consequential amendment by repealing the Ofsted/Estyn duty to inspect LEA accessibility strategies and plans made under the Disability Discrimination Act 1995. These plans can now be inspected under the amended s.38 of the 1997 Act.

It is expected that this provision will commence on 1 June 2005.

52 Duty of local authorities to promote educational achievement

In section 22 of the Children Act 1989 (c. 41) (general duty of local authority in relation to children looked after by them), after subsection (3) insert-
  "(3A) The duty of a local authority under subsection (3)(a) to safeguard and promote the welfare of a child looked after by them includes in particular a duty to promote the child's educational achievement."

Local authorities have a duty under s.22(3) of the Children Act 1989 to safeguard and promote the welfare of children they are looking after. A new subsection (3A) is added to require the local authority, as the corporate parent, to promote the educational achievement of looked after children. In other words, the local authority must consider the implications for the education of children in care when making care arrangements. In spite of several attempts, the Government resisted

53 Ascertaining children's wishes

(1) In section 17 of the Children Act 1989 (provision of services to children), after subsection (4) insert–
"(4A) Before determining what (if any) services to provide for a particular child in need in the exercise of functions conferred on them by this section, a local authority shall, so far as is reasonably practicable and consistent with the child's welfare-
  (a) ascertain the child's wishes and feelings regarding the provision of those services; and
  (b) give due consideration (having regard to his age and understanding) to such wishes and feelings of the child as they have been able to ascertain."

(2) In section 20 of that Act (provision of accommodation for children: general), in subsection (6)(a) and (b), after "wishes" insert "and feelings".

(3) In section 47 of that Act (local authority's duty to investigate), after subsection (5) insert–
"(5A) For the purposes of making a determination under this section as to the action to be taken with respect to a child, a local authority shall, so far as is reasonably practicable and consistent with the child's welfare–
  (a) ascertain the child's wishes and feelings regarding the action to be taken with respect to him; and
  (b) give due consideration (having regard to his age and understanding) to such wishes and feelings of the child as they have been able to ascertain."

54 Information about individual children

In section 83 of the Children Act 1989 (research and returns of information), after subsection (4) insert-

---

placing a similar duty on school governing bodies.

Section 17 (Provision of services for children in need, their families and others) of the Children Act 1989 requires local authorities to safeguard and promote the welfare of children in need in their areas by providing suitable services. A new subsection (4A) is added, which gives statutory backing to existing guidance: local authorities must ascertain a child's wishes and feelings, consistent with the child's age and understanding, before providing suitable services.

Section 20 (Provision of accommodation for children: general) of the Children Act 1989 is amended to require a local authority to ascertain a child's 'feelings' before providing, or not providing, accommodation. Local authorities are already under a duty to ascertain a child's 'wishes'.

Section 47 (Local authority's duty to investigate) of the Children Act 1989 provides the local authority duty to investigate the circumstances of a child prior to applying to the courts for an order or exercising any of its powers under the 1989 Act. A new subsection (5A) is added, which requires local authorities to find out a child's wishes and feelings about possible local authorities services and give consideration to those wishes before taking action.

The Secretary of State and NAfW can require local authorities and

"(4A) Particulars required to be transmitted under subsection (3) or (4) may include particulars relating to and identifying individual children."

voluntary organisations to return specified information under subsections (3) and (4) of s.83 (Research and information) of the Children Act 1989. The new subsection (4A) inserted by this section allows particulars of individual children to be submitted. The Explanatory Notes state particular information on individual children will be used 'for statistical analysis in order to inform and review policy about children and young people. It will also be used to ensure that local practitioners have all the relevant and accurate information they need to carry out their functions'.

55 Social services committees

(1) Sections 2 to 5 of the Local Authority Social Services Act 1970 (c. 42) (social services committees) shall cease to have effect.

The local governance arrangements for social services functions are amended to bring the law up to date with current practice. The following provisions of the Local Authority Social Services Act 1970 are repealed: duty to establish a social services committee (s.2 – but see subsection (5) below), delegation of business by local authorities to social services committees (s.3 and 3A), joint committees with other local authorities (s.4) and membership of committees (s.5). Schedule 5, Part 4, repeals references to social services committees and social services departments found in 11 other Acts. References to social services departments are removed as a consequence of requiring a Director of Children's Services and a Director of Adult Social Services.

(2) In Schedule 1 to that Act (enactments conferring functions assigned to social services committees), for the heading substitute "SOCIAL SERVICES FUNCTIONS".

A consequential amendment to the 1970 Act.

(3) In section 63(8) of the Health Services and Public Health Act 1968 (c. 46) (instruction), in paragraph (a) of the definition of "relevant enactments", for the words from "for the time being" to "section 2" substitute "are social services functions within the meaning".

A consequential amendment relating to health functions.

(4) In Schedule 1 to the Local Government and Housing Act 1989 (c. 42) (political balance on committees), in paragraph 4(1), in paragraph (a) of the definition of "ordinary committee", for the words from "the authority's" to "any other committee" substitute "any committee".

Removes the reference to the social services committee in committees that are required to be politically balanced.

(5) In section 102 of the Local Government Act 2000 (c. 22) (social services functions)-
 (a) omit subsection (1);
 (b) in subsection (2), for "that Act" substitute "the Local Authority Social Services Act 1970".

Removes the requirement on local authorities that do not have executive arrangement under the Local Government Act 2000 to have a social services committee. Such authorities can have other arrangements to exercise social services functions.

56 Social services functions

In Schedule 1 to the Local Authority Social Services Act 1970 (c. 42) (functions which are social services functions), at the end insert-

| "Children Act 2004 Sections 13 to 16 and 31 to 34 | Functions relating to Local Safeguarding Children Boards." |

Sections 13 to 16 and 31 to 34, which are the CSA functions relating to LSCBs, are made social services functions by insertion of references to these sections in Schedule 1 of the Local Authority Social Services Act 1970. One implication is that the LSCBs will be open to inspections by the Commission for Social Care Inspection.

Other provisions

57 Fees payable to adoption review panel members

In section 12 of the Adoption and Children Act 2002 (c. 38) (independent review of determinations), in subsection (3)(d) (power to make provision as to the payment of expenses of members of a panel) for "expenses of" substitute "fees to".

Section 12 of the Adoption and Children Act 2002 provides for reviews of adoption agency decisions to turn down prospective adopters. Ministers delegate decisions about reviews to review panels. The amendment to s.12 ensures that panel members can be paid fees for their work and not

58 Reasonable punishment

(1) In relation to any offence specified in subsection (2), battery of a child cannot be justified on the ground that it constituted reasonable punishment.

Removes most defences that a parent, or someone acting as a parent, can use in criminal proceedings to justify child battery (sometimes called reasonable chastisement or reasonable punishment) when charged with a criminal offence listed in subsection (2).

(2) The offences referred to in subsection (1) are-
   (a) an offence under section 18 or 20 of the Offences against the Person Act 1861 (c. 100) (wounding and causing grievous bodily harm);
   (b) an offence under section 47 of that Act (assault occasioning actual bodily harm);
   (c) an offence under section 1 of the Children and Young Persons Act 1933 (c. 12) (cruelty to persons under 16).

The criminal offences referred to in subsection (1).

(3) Battery of a child causing actual bodily harm to the child cannot be justified in any civil proceedings on the ground that it constituted reasonable punishment.

Prevents child battery that causes 'actual bodily harm' being used as a defence in civil proceedings. The definition of 'actual bodily harm' in civil proceedings is the same as that used in criminal proceedings, that is an assault or battery that causes any injury that is calculated to interfere with the health or comfort of the victim.

(4) For the purposes of subsection (3) "actual bodily harm" has the same meaning as it has for the purposes of section 47 of the Offences against the Person Act 1861.

Defines 'actual bodily harm'.

(5) In section 1 of the Children and Young Persons Act 1933, omit subsection (7).

Removes the offence in section 1 of the Children and Young Person Act 1933.

59 Power to give financial assistance

(1) Section 14 of the Education Act 2002 (c. 32) (power of Secretary of State and Assembly to give financial

Section 14 of the Education Act 2002, which gives wide powers to

[sidebar top: just expenses. The alteration will bring payments to review panel members into line with payments to adoption panel members.]

assistance for purposes related to education or childcare) is amended as specified in subsections (2) to (4).

the Secretary of State or Assembly to fund education activities made by local authorities or otherwise, is amended.

(2) In subsection (2) of that section (purposes for which assistance may be given), at the end insert-
"(j) the promotion of the welfare of children and their parents;
(k) the provision of support for parenting (including support for prospective parents)."

The funding power is extended to include welfare of children and support for parenting.

(3) After that subsection insert-
"(2A) In subsection (2)(j), "children" means persons under the age of twenty."

'Children' is defined as persons under the age of 20.

(4) In the heading to that section, for "childcare" substitute "children etc".

Technical (changes section title).

(5) In the heading to Part 2 of that Act, for "childcare" substitute "children etc".

Technical (changes Part title).

60 Child safety orders

(1) The Crime and Disorder Act 1998 (c. 37) is amended as follows.

Amends s. 8 (Parenting Orders), s. 11 (Child Safety Orders) and s. 12 (Child Safety Orders: supplemental) of the Crime and Disorder Act 1998.

(2) In section 8(1)(a) (power to make parenting order where a child safety order is made), at the end insert "or the court determines on an application under section 12(6) below that a child has failed to comply with any requirement included in such an order".

Creates an additional circumstance in which a court can make a parenting order under s.12, namely where the child has failed to comply with a child safety order under s. 8.

(3) In section 11(4) (maximum period permitted for child safety orders), for the words from "three months" to the end substitute "twelve months".

Extends the maximum period for a child safety order from 3 months to 12 months.

(4) In section 12, omit subsections (6)(a) and (7) (power to make care order on breach of child safety order).

Removes from the courts the power to make a care order at a lower threshold than that required by s.31 (care and supervision orders) of the Children Act 1989.

61 Children's Commissioner for Wales: powers of entry

In the Care Standards Act 2000 (c. 14), in section 76 (further functions of Children's Commissioner for Wales), at the end insert-

"(8) The Commissioner or a person authorised by him may for the purposes of any function of the Commissioner under section 72B or 73 or subsection (4) of this section at any reasonable time-
  (a) enter any premises, other than a private dwelling, for the purposes of interviewing any child accommodated or cared for there; and
  (b) if the child consents, interview the child in private."

Gives the Children's Commissioner for Wales similar powers of entry to interview children to those enjoyed by the Children's Commissioner in s. 2(8) when carrying out inquiries. The Children's Commissioner for Wales has no powers of entry where there are not similar powers held by the Children's Commissioner. For example, the Children's Commissioner for Wales has a power to examine individual cases under s. 74 of the Care Standards Act 2000. This is a power not held by the Children's Commissioner and no powers of entry are granted by this section.

62 Publication of material relating to legal proceedings

(1) In section 97(2) of the Children Act 1989 (c. 41) (privacy for children involved in certain proceedings), after "publish" insert "to the public at large or any section of the public".

Section 97 (Privacy for children involved in certain proceedings) of the Children Act 1989 prevents the publication of any material likely to identify a child who is subject to any legal proceedings under the Act. This absolute prohibition of disclosure has been subject to adverse comment because of it preventing professional discussions. This subsection amends the 1989 Act to make it clear that the absolute prohibition extends only to publication of information 'to the public at large or any section of the public'. It is envisaged that the various court rules will be amended to take account of this change and subsections (3) to (7) are consequential amendments to the various powers to produce court rules.

(2) In section 12(4) of the Administration of Justice Act 1960 (c. 65) (publication of information relating to proceedings in private), at the end insert "(and in par-

Makes it clear there can be no contempt if a court authorises publication of information.

ticular where the publication is not so punishable by reason of being authorised by rules of court)".

(3) In section 66 of the Adoption Act 1976 (c. 36) (rules of procedure), after subsection (5) insert-
"(5A) Rules may, for the purposes of the law relating to contempt of court, authorise the publication in such circumstances as may be specified of information relating to proceedings held in private involving children."

This is a consequential section relating to adoption proceedings.

(4) In section 145(1) of the Magistrates' Courts Act 1980 (c. 43) (rules: supplementary), after paragraph (g) insert-
"(ga) authorising, for the purposes of the law relating to contempt of court, the publication in such circumstances as may be specified of information relating to proceedings referred to in section 12(1)(a) of the Administration of Justice Act 1960 which are held in private;".

This is a consequential section relating to Magistrates' Court rules.

(5) In section 40(4) of the Matrimonial and Family Proceedings Act 1984 (c. 42) (family proceedings rules), in paragraph (a) after "County Courts Act 1984;" insert-
"(aa) authorise, for the purposes of the law relating to contempt of court, the publication in such circumstances as may be specified of information relating to family proceedings held in private;".

This is a consequential section relating to the Family Proceedings Rules.

(6) In section 141 of the Adoption and Children Act 2002 (c. 38) (rules of procedure) at the end insert-
"(6) Rules may, for the purposes of the law relating to contempt of court, authorise the publication in such circumstances as may be specified of information relating to proceedings held in private involving children."

This is a consequential section relating to rules made under the Adoption and Children Act 2002.

(7) In section 76 of the Courts Act 2003 (c. 39) (Family Procedure Rules: further provision) after subsection (2) insert-
"(2A) Family Procedure Rules may, for the purposes of the law relating to contempt of court, authorise the publication in such circumstances as may be specified of information relating to family proceedings held in private."

This is a consequential section relating to the Family Procedure Rules.

63 Disclosure of information by Inland Revenue

(1) In Schedule 5 to the Tax Credits Act 2002 (c. 21) (use and disclosure of information), after paragraph 10 insert-

"Provision of information by Board for purposes relating to welfare of children

10A (1) This paragraph applies to information, other than information relating to a person's income, which is held for the purposes of functions relating to tax credits, child benefit or guardian's allowance-
- (a) by the Board, or
- (b) by a person providing services to the Board, in connection with the provision of those services.

(2) Information to which this paragraph applies may be supplied to-
- (a) a local authority in England and Wales for use for the purpose of any enquiry or investigation under Part 5 of the Children Act 1989 relating to the welfare of a child;
- (b) a local authority in Scotland for use for the purpose of any enquiry or investigation under Chapter 3 of Part 2 of the Children (Scotland) Act 1995 relating to the welfare of a child;
- (c) an authority in Northern Ireland for use for the purpose of any enquiry or investigation under Part 6 of the Children (Northern Ireland) Order 1995 (S.I. 1995/755 (N.I.2)) relating to the welfare of a child.

(3) Information supplied under this paragraph is not to be supplied by the recipient to any other person or body unless it is supplied-
- (a) for the purpose of any enquiry or investigation referred to in sub-paragraph (2) above,
- (b) for the purpose of civil or criminal proceedings, or
- (c) where paragraph (a) or (b) does not apply, to a person to whom the information could be supplied directly by or under the authority of the Board.

(4) Information may not be supplied under sub-paragraph (3)(b) or (c) without the authority of the Board.

Amends the Tax Credits Act 2002 to allow the Inland Revenue to disclose information about a person's tax credits, child benefit or guardian's allowance, but not income, to a local authority in England and Wales (and their equivalents in Scotland and Northern Ireland) for enquiries and investigations about the welfare of a child under Part 5 of the Children Act 1989. Information can be passed on to other bodies, for example the police, without the consent of the Inland Revenue, when related to the local authority's investigation. The Inland Revenue must give consent if the information is passed on for other purposes, such as the bringing of civil or criminal proceedings. An offence can be committed for wrongful disclosure of information.

(5) A person commits an offence if he discloses information supplied to him under this paragraph unless the disclosure is made-
(a) in accordance with sub-paragraph (3),
(b) in accordance with an enactment or an order of a court,
(c) with consent given by or on behalf of the person to whom the information relates, or
(d) in such a way as to prevent the identification of the person to whom it relates.

(6) It is a defence for a person charged with an offence under subparagraph (5) to prove that he reasonably believed that his disclosure was lawful.

(7) A person guilty of an offence under sub-paragraph (5) is liable-
(a) on conviction on indictment, to imprisonment for a term not exceeding two years, to a fine or to both;
(b) on summary conviction in England and Wales, to imprisonment for a term not exceeding twelve months, to a fine not exceeding the statutory maximum or to both;
(c) on summary conviction in Scotland or Northern Ireland, to imprisonment for a funded term not exceeding six months, to a fine not exceeding the statutory maximum or to both.

(8) In sub-paragraph (2) "child" means a person under the age of eighteen and-
(a) in paragraph (a), "local authority" has the meaning given by section 105(1) of the Children Act 1989;
(b) in paragraph (b), "local authority" has the meaning given by section 93(1) of the Children (Scotland) Act 1995; and
(c) in paragraph (c), "authority" has the meaning given by Article 2 of the Children (Northern Ireland) Order 1995 (S.I. 1995/755 (N.I.2)).

(9) The reference to an enactment in sub-paragraph (5)(b) includes a reference to an enactment comprised in, or in an instrument made under, an Act of the Scottish Parliament."

(2) In relation to an offence committed under sub-paragraph (5) of paragraph 10A of Schedule 5 to the Tax Credits Act 2002 (c. 21) (as inserted by subsection (1) above) before the commencement of section 154 of the Criminal Justice Act 2003, the reference in sub-paragraph (7)(b) of that paragraph to twelve months shall be read as a reference to six months.

Provision awaiting the commencement of s. 154 of the Criminal Justice Act 2003.

Part 6 General

This part makes a number of necessary technical points.

64 Repeals

The enactments specified in Schedule 5 are repealed to the extent specified.

Adds Schedule 5, which collects repeals of earlier legislation arising from this Act as follows:
- *Part 1 – Children and Young People's Plans (ss 17 and 26)*
- *Part 2 – Child Minding and Day Care (s. 48 and schedule 4)*
- *Part 3 – Inspection of local education authorities (s. 51)*
- *Part 4 – Reasonable punishment (s. 58)*
- *Part 5 – Child Safety Orders (s.60)*

65 Interpretation

(1) In this Act–
"the Assembly" means the National Assembly for Wales;
"child" means, subject to section 9, a person under the age of eighteen (and "children" is to be construed accordingly);
"children's services authority in England" means-
(a) a county council in England;
(b) a metropolitan district council;
(c) a non-metropolitan district council for an area for which there is no county council;
(d) a London borough council;
(e) the Common Council of the City of London;
(f) the Council of the Isles of Scilly; "children's services authority in Wales" means a county council or county borough council in Wales.

Defines:
- *the Assembly – National Assembly for Wales (NAfW)*
- *Child – a person under the age of 18*
- *Children's Services Authority – a local authority that has education and social services responsibilities in England and Wales.*

(2) This Act applies in relation to the Isles of Scilly subject to such modifications as may be specified by order made by the Secretary of State.

Applies the Act to the Isles of Scilly, subject to modifications specified by the Secretary of State.

(3) In this Act-
  (a) references to a prison include a young offender institution;
  (b) references to a contracted out secure training centre, and to the contractor in relation to such a secure training centre, have the meanings given by section 15 of the Criminal Justice and Public Order Act 1994 (c. 33);
  (c) references to a contracted out prison, and to the contractor in relation to such a prison, have the meanings given by section 84(4) of the Criminal Justice Act 1991 (c. 53).

Further definitions:
- *'Prison' includes young offender institutions*
- *'Contracted out secure training centre' is defined in the Criminal Justice and Public Order Act 1994*
- *'Contracted out prison' is defined in the Criminal Justice Act 1991.*

(4) Where-
  (a) a contract under section 7 of the Criminal Justice and Public Order Act 1994 is for the time being in force in relation to part of a secure training centre, or
  (b) a contract under section 84 of the Criminal Justice Act 1991 is for the time being in force in relation to part of a prison,
this Act has effect as if each part of the secure training centre or prison were a separate institution.

Requires the private provider of part of the provision at a secure training centre or prison to safeguard and promote the welfare of children and be represented of the LSCB.

66 Regulations and orders

(1) Any power to make regulations or an order under this Act includes power-
  (a) to make different provision for different purposes;
  (b) to make different provision for different cases or areas;
  (c) to make incidental, supplementary, consequential or transitional provision or savings.

Standard provision relating to the making of regulations and orders.

(2) Any power to make regulations or an order under this Act, other than an order under section 42 or 43, is exercisable by statutory instrument.

Regulations and orders have to be made by statutory instrument, that is a formal document laid before Parliament, except orders under ss. 42 or 43, which transfer CAFCASS property and staff to the NAfW.

(3) The Secretary of State may not make a statutory instrument containing regulations under section 12 or 45 unless a draft of the instrument has been laid before, and approved by resolution of, each House of Parliament.

In England, regulations on information databases and the registration scheme orf private foster carers have to be approved by the 'affirmative resolution' procedure with each House of Parliament approving the regulations.

(4) The Secretary of State may not make a statutory instrument containing the first order under section 49 unless a draft of the instrument has been laid before, and approved by resolution of, each House of Parliament.

The first use of the order making power on payments to foster parents (s. 49) requires an affirmative resolution.

(5) A statutory instrument containing-
   (a) any regulations made by the Secretary of State under this Act to which subsection (3) does not apply,
   (b) an order made by the Secretary of State under section 49 to which subsection (4) does not apply, or
   (c) an order made by the Secretary of State under section 11(1)(d) or section 65(2),
is subject to annulment in pursuance of a resolution of either House of Parliament.

Other statutory instruments containing regulations have to be approved by the 'negative resolution' procedure, that is the instrument has to be laid before Parliament but can be negated by a resolution of either House of Parliament, which is a very rare occurrence.

(6) Subsection (5) does not apply to regulations made by the Secretary of State jointly with the Assembly under section 43(7).

Regulations jointly made by the Secretary of State and the NAfW on consultation on the transfer of CAFCASS staff to the Assembly are not subject to the negative resolution procedure.

67 Commencement

(1) Part 1 comes into force on the day on which this Act is passed.

The Children's Commissioner law came into effect on Royal Assent.

(2) Part 2 comes into force in accordance with provision made by order by the Secretary of State.

The Children's Services in England law comes into force by order of the Secretary of State.

(3) Part 3 comes into force in accordance with provision made by order by the Assembly subject to subsections (4) and (5).

The Children's Services in Wales law comes into force by order of the National Assembly for Wales except where the consent of, or consultation with, the Secretary of State is required for non-devolved matters and other matters listed in subsections (4) and (5).

(4) The Assembly must obtain the consent of the Secretary of State before making provision under subsection (3) in relation to section 25(4)(a) to (c) or 31(3)(a) to (c), (f) or (g).

The Assembly must seek the consent of the Secretary of State before commencing the provisions on cooperation and LSCBs that involve non-devolved bodies.

(5) In section 28, the following provisions come into force in accordance with provision made by order by the Secretary of State after consulting the Assembly-
   (a) subsection (1)(d) to (h);
   (b) subsection (2), so far as relating to the persons and bodies referred to in subsection (1)(d) to (h);
   (c) subsection (5).

The Assembly must consult the Secretary of State before making regulations on information sharing.

(6) Part 4 comes into force in accordance with provision made by order by the Assembly with the consent of the Secretary of State.

The transfer of CAFCASS to Wales comes into force by order of the NAfW with the consent of the Secretary of State.

(7) In Part 5-
   (a) section 44 so far as relating to England comes into force in accordance with provision made by order by the Secretary of State, and so far as relating to Wales in accordance with provision made by order by the Assembly;
   (b) sections 45 to 47 come into force at the end of the period of two months beginning with the day on which this Act is passed;
   (c) section 48 and Schedule 4 so far as relating to England come into force in accordance with provision made by order by the Secretary of State, and so far as relating to Wales in accordance with provision made by order by the Assembly;
   (d) section 49 comes into force at the end of the period of two months beginning with the day on which this Act is passed;
   (e) sections 50 to 57 so far as relating to England come into force in accordance with provision made by order by the Secretary of State, and so far as relating to Wales in accordance with provision made by order by the Assembly;
   (f) section 58 comes into force at the end of the period of two months beginning with the day on which this Act is passed;
   (g) section 59 comes into force on the day on which this Act is passed;
   (h) section 60 comes into force in accordance with provision made by order by the Secretary of State;
   (i) section 61 comes into force in accordance with provision made by order by the Assembly;
   (j) section 62 comes into force in accordance with provision made by order by the Lord Chancellor;

- *The amended law of private fostering (s. 44) comes into force by order of the Secretary of State for England and NAfW for Wales.*
- *The law on the new private fostering registration scheme (ss 45 to 47) comes into force two months after the enactment (15 January 2005), although regulations are required to implement the scheme.*
- *The amended law on child minding and day care (s. 48 and schedule 4) comes into force by order of the Secretary of State and NAfW.*
- *The new law on payments to foster parents (s. 49) comes into force two months after the enactment (15 January 2005) although an order is required to specify a scheme of payments.*
- *The law on local authority services (ss 50 to 57) comes into force by order of the Secretary of State for England and NAfW for Wales.*
- *The law on reasonable punishment (s. 59) comes into force two months after Royal Assent.*
- *Widening the power to give financial assistance (s. 59) comes into force on Royal Assent.*
- *The amended law on child safety orders (s. 60) comes into force by order of the Secretary of State.*

(k) section 63 comes into force on the day on which this Act is passed.

- The power of entry for the Children's Commissioner for Wales (s. 61) comes into force by order of the Assembly.
- The new law on publication of material related to legal proceedings (s. 62) comes into force by order of the Lord Chancellor.
- The law on Inland Revenue disclosures (s. 63) comes into force on Royal Assent.

(8) This Part comes into force on the day on which this Act is passed except that Schedule 5 comes into force in accordance with the commencement provisions set out in that Schedule.

This Part comes into force on Royal Assent, except Schedule 5.

68 Extent

(1) Part 1 extends to the whole of the United Kingdom (unless otherwise specifically provided).

The Children's Commissioner role extends to the whole of the UK as defined in Part 1.

(2) Parts 2 to 4 extend to England and Wales only.

The law on children's services, CAFCASS transfer and miscellaneous provisions extends only to England and Wales.

(3) In Part 5-
 (a) sections 44 to 62 extend to England and Wales only;
 (b) section 63 extends to the whole of the United Kingdom.

All of Part 5 extends to England and Wales only except s. 63 (Reasonable punishment), which extends to the whole UK.

(4) In this Part-
 (a) section 64 and Schedule 5 extend to England and Wales only; and
 (b) the remaining provisions extend to the whole of the United Kingdom.

Part 6 extends to the whole UK except for the repeals (s. 64 and Schedule 5).

69 Short title

This Act may be cited as the Children Act 2004.

The short title of the Act is Children Act 2004. The Act is not an education act.

Schedule 1   Children's Commissioner

See section 1. Contains standard provisions relating to non-departmental public bodies including the appointment of the chief officer (Children's Commissioner), powers, remuneration, staffing, accounts and pensions. Of note are the following:
- although appointed by the Secretary of State, the Secretary of State must involve children in the appointment of the Children's Commissioner (paragraph 1(1) and (2))
- the Children's Commissioner's appointment is for a maximum period of five years and is only eligible for reappointment once (paragraph 1(4) and (5)
- there must be a deputy Children's Commissioner (paragraph 5(1))
- although the Children's Commissioner will not have Crown immunity (paragraph1(2)), statements made by the Children's Commissioner in a published report will have absolute privilege for the purposes of the law defamation and any other statement will have qualified privilege (paragraph 10).

Status

1   (1)   The Children's Commissioner is to be a corporation sole.
    (2)   The Children's Commissioner is not to be regarded as the servant or agent of the Crown or as enjoying any status, immunity or privilege of the Crown; and his property is not to be regarded as property of, or property held on behalf of, the Crown.

General powers

2   (1)   The Children's Commissioner may do anything which appears to him to be necessary or expedient for the purpose of, or in connection with, the exercise of his functions.

    (2)   In particular he may-
          (a) co-operate with other public authorities in the United Kingdom;
          (b) enter into contracts; and
          (c) acquire, hold and dispose of any property.

Appointment and tenure of office

3   (1)   The Children's Commissioner is to be appointed by the Secretary of State.

    (2)   The Secretary of State must, to such extent and in such manner as he thinks fit, involve children in the appointment of the Children's Commissioner.

    (3)   Subject to the provisions of this paragraph, a person shall hold and vacate office as the Children's Commissioner in accordance with the terms and conditions of his appointment as determined by the Secretary of State.

(4) An appointment as the Children's Commissioner shall be for a term not exceeding five years.

(5) A person who has held office as the Children's Commissioner is eligible for reappointment once only.

(6) The Children's Commissioner may at any time resign by notice in writing to the Secretary of State.

(7) The Secretary of State may remove the Children's Commissioner from office if he is satisfied that he has-
   (a) become unfit or unable properly to discharge his functions; or
   (b) behaved in a way that is not compatible with his continuing in office.

Remuneration

4   The Secretary of State must-
   (a) pay the Children's Commissioner such remuneration and allowances, and
   (b) pay or make provision for the payment of such pension or gratuities to or in respect of him,
as may be provided under the terms of his appointment.

Staff

5 (1) The Children's Commissioner may appoint any staff he considers necessary for assisting him in the exercise of his functions, one of whom shall be appointed as deputy Children's Commissioner.

(2) During any vacancy in the office of Children's Commissioner or at any time when the Children's Commissioner is for any reason unable to act, the deputy Children's Commissioner shall exercise his functions (and any property or rights vested in the Children's Commissioner may accordingly be dealt with by the deputy Children's Commissioner as if vested in him).

(3) Without prejudice to sub-paragraph (2), any member of the Children's Commissioner's staff may, so far as authorised by him, exercise any of his functions.

Pensions

6 (1) In the Superannuation Act 1972 (c. 11), in Schedule 1 (kinds of employment etc to which section 1 of that Act applies)-
   (a) in the list of "Other Bodies", at the end insert "Employment by the Children's Commissioner";
   (b) in the list of "Offices", at the appropriate place insert "Children's Commissioner".

(2) The Secretary of State must pay to the Minister for the Civil Service, at such times as the Minister may direct, such sums as he may determine in respect of any increase attributable to sub-paragraph (1) in the sums payable out of money provided by Parliament under the Superannuation Act 1972.

Funding

7   The Secretary of State may make payments to the Children's Commissioner of such amounts, at such times and on such conditions (if any) as the Secretary of State considers appropriate.

Accounts

8   (1) The Children's Commissioner must-
   (a) keep proper accounting records;
   (b) prepare a statement of accounts for each financial year; and
   (c) send a copy of each such statement of accounts to the Secretary of State and the Comptroller and Auditor General as soon as possible after the end of the financial year to which the statement relates.

   (2) The Comptroller and Auditor General must examine, certify and report on each statement of accounts sent to him under sub-paragraph (1)(c) and must lay copies of the statement and of his report before Parliament.

   (3) In this paragraph, "financial year" means-
   (a) the period beginning with the date on which the first Children's Commissioner is appointed and ending with 31st March next following that date; and
   (b) each successive period of twelve months ending with 31st March.

Evidence

9   (1) A document purporting to be duly executed under the seal of the Children's Commissioner or to be signed by him or on his behalf is to be received in evidence and, unless the contrary is proved, taken to be so executed or signed.

   (2) This paragraph does not extend to Scotland.

Protection from defamation actions

10   For the purposes of the law of defamation-
   (a) any statement made by the Children's Commissioner in a report published under this Part has absolute privilege; and
   (b) any other statement made by the Children's Commissioner or a member of his staff for the purposes of this Part has qualified privilege.

Regulated position

11 In the Criminal Justice and Court Services Act 2000 (c. 43), in section 36(6) (meaning of "regulated position"), after paragraph (f) insert-
"(fa) Children's Commissioner and deputy Children's Commissioner appointed under Part 1 of the Children Act 2004,".

Disqualifications

12 In the House of Commons Disqualification Act 1975 (c. 24), in Part 3 of Schedule 1 (certain disqualifying offices), at the appropriate places insert the following entries-
"Children's Commissioner";
"Member of staff of the Children's Commissioner".

13 In the Northern Ireland Assembly Disqualification Act 1975 (c. 25), in Part 3 of Schedule 1 (certain disqualifying offices), at the appropriate places insert the following entries-
"Children's Commissioner";
"Member of staff of the Children's Commissioner".

Schedule 2 Director of children's services: consequential amendments

Children and Young Persons Act 1933 (c. 12)

1   In section 96 of the Children and Young Persons Act 1933 (provisions as to local authorities), in subsection (8), for "or the chief education officer of the authority" substitute "of the authority, the director of children's services (in the case of an authority in England) or the chief education officer (in the case of an authority in Wales)".

Enables the Director of Children's Services to represent the local authority, if the local authority so wishes, in childcare cases that appear to the Director to be urgent.

Local Authority Social Services Act 1970 (c. 42)

2   (1) The Local Authority Social Services Act 1970 is amended as follows.

       (2) In section 6 (director of social services)-
            (a) before subsection (1) insert-
                 "(A1) A local authority in England shall appoint an officer, to be known as the director of adult social services, for the purposes of their social services functions, other than those for which the authority's director of children's services is responsible under section 18 of the Children Act 2004.";
            (b) in subsection (1), after "local authority" insert "in Wales";
            (c) in subsection (2), after "director of", in both places, insert "adult social services or (as the case may be)";
            (d) in subsection (6), for "a director of social services" substitute "a person under this section".

Removes the duty on a local authority in England to appoint a Director of Social Services and substitutes a Director of Adult Social Services while not changing the law in Wales.

       (3) In Schedule 1, in the entry for "Sections 6 and 7B of this Act", after the words "Appointment of" insert "director of adult social services or".

Local Government and Housing Act 1989 (c. 42)

3 In section 2 of the Local Government and Housing Act 1989 (politically restricted posts), in subsection (6)-
 (a) after "means-" insert-
  "(za) the director of children's services appointed under section 18 of the Children Act 2004 and the director of adult social services appointed under section 6(A1) of the Local Authority Social Services Act 1970 (in the case of a local authority in England);";
 (b) in paragraph (a), at the end insert "(in the case of a local authority in Wales)";
 (c) in paragraph (c) after "director of social services" insert "(in the case of a local authority in Wales)".

Makes the Director of Children's Services and Director of Adult Social Services into politically restricted posts.

Education Act 1996 (c. 56)

4 (1) The Education Act 1996 is amended as follows.

 (2) In section 532 (appointment of chief education officer), for "A local authority's duties" substitute "The duties of a local education authority in Wales".

 (3) In section 566 (evidence: documents), in subsection (1)(a), for "chief education officer of that authority" substitute "director of children's services (in the case of an authority in England) or the chief education officer (in the case of an authority in Wales)".

Restricts the duty to appoint a chief education officer to an LEA in Wales, and amends the law on authorising documents so that the Director of Children's Services will, in future, carry out the role of the chief education officer in authorising documents.

Crime and Disorder Act 1998 (c. 37)

5 (1) The Crime and Disorder Act 1998 is amended as follows.

 (2) In section 8 (responsible officers in relation to parenting orders), in subsection (8)(bb),

Enables the Director of Children's Services to nominate officers to make applications for parenting orders. Also requires the Director of Children's Services to nominate

after "nominated by" insert "a person appointed as director of children's services under section 18 of the Children Act 2004 or by".

(3) In section 39 (youth offending teams), in subsection (5)-
  (a) after paragraph (a) insert-
    "(aa) where the local authority is in England, a person with experience of social work in relation to children nominated by the director of children's services appointed by the local authority under section 18 of the Children Act 2004;";
  (b) in paragraph (b) for "a social worker of a" substitute "where the local authority is in Wales, a social worker of the";
  (c) after paragraph (d) insert-
    "(da) where the local authority is in England, a person with experience in education nominated by the director of children's services appointed by the local authority under section 18 of the Children Act 2004;";
  (d) in paragraph (e) insert at the beginning "where the local authority is in Wales,".

one person with social work and one person with education experience for membership of the youth offending team.

Protection of Children Act 1999 (c. 14)

6   In section 4C of the Protection of Children Act 1999 (restoration to the list) in subsection (1), for "director of social services of a local authority" substitute "director of children's services of a local authority in England or a director of social services of a local authority in Wales".

Enables the Director of Children's Services to apply to the High Court to have the name of an individual restored to the list of those considered unsuitable to work with children in order to protect children.

Criminal Justice and Court Services Act 2000 (c. 43)

7   (1)   The Criminal Justice and Court Services Act 2000 is amended as follows.

     (2)   In section 34 (restoration of disqualification order), in subsection (1), for "a director of social services of a local authority" substitute "a director of children's services of a local authority in England or a director of social services of a local authority in Wales".

     (3)   In section 36 (meaning of "regulated position"), in subsection (6)-
- (a) after paragraph (b) insert-
  - "(ba) director of children's services and director of adult social services of a local authority in England,";
- (b) in paragraph (c) at the end insert "in Wales";
- (c) in paragraph (d) at the end insert "in Wales".

Makes the Director of Children's Services and the Director of Adult Social Services into 'regulated positions'. Not only must the post holders not be disqualified from working with children, it will be a criminal offence for a disqualified individual to apply for such a position.

Criminal Justice Act 2003 (c. 44)

8   In section 322 of the Criminal Justice Act 2003 (individual support orders), in the new section 1AA to be inserted in the Crime and Disorder Act 1998 (c. 37), in subsection (10)(b), after "nominated by" insert "a person appointed as director of children's services under section 18 of the Children Act 2004 or by".

A person nominated by the Director of Children's Services can be a 'responsible officer' for the purposes of individual support orders. The new order was available from 1 May 2004 for 10 to 17 year-olds with anti-social behaviour orders.

Schedule 3 Advisory and support services for family proceedings

See section 40. Makes consequential amendments to the transfer of CAFCASS functions in Wales to the National Assembly for Wales.

Domestic Proceedings and Magistrates' Courts Act 1978 (c. 22)

1   In section 26 of the Domestic Proceedings and Magistrates' Courts Act 1978 (reconciliation), in subsection (2), after "Criminal Justice and Court Services Act 2000)" insert ", a Welsh family proceedings officer (within the meaning given by section 35 of the Children Act 2004)".

Child Abduction and Custody Act 1985 (c. 60)

2   The Child Abduction and Custody Act 1985 is amended as follows.

3   In sections 6(a) and 21(a) (reports), after "an officer of the Service" insert "or a Welsh family proceedings officer".

4   In section 27 (interpretation), after subsection (5) insert-
"(5A)   In this Act "Welsh family proceedings officer" has the meaning given by section 35 of the Children Act 2004".

Children Act 1989 (c. 41)

5   The Children Act 1989 is amended as follows.

6   In section 7 (welfare reports), in subsections (1)(a) and (b) and (5), after "an officer of the Service" insert "or a Welsh family proceedings officer".

7   In section 16 (family assistance orders), in subsection (1), after "an officer of the Service" insert "or a Welsh family proceedings officer".

8   (1)   Section 26 (review of cases etc) is amended as follows.

           (2)   In subsection (2A)(c) after "Service" insert "or a Welsh family proceedings officer".

           (3)   After subsection (2C) insert-
"(2D)   The power to make regulations in subsection (2C) is exercisable in relation to functions of Welsh family proceedings offi-

cers only with the consent of the National Assembly for Wales."

9 (1) Section 41 (representation of child) is amended as follows.

   (2) In subsection (1), after "an officer of the Service" insert "or a Welsh family proceedings officer".

   (3) In subsections (2) and (4)(a), after "officer of the Service" insert "or Welsh family proceedings officer".

   (4) In subsection (10)-
       (a) in paragraphs (a) and (b), after "officer of the Service" insert "or Welsh family proceedings officer";
       (b) in paragraph (c), after "officers of the Service" insert "or Welsh family proceedings officers".

   (5) In subsection (11), after "an officer of the Service" insert "or a Welsh family proceedings officer".

10 In section 42 (rights of officers of the Service), in subsections (1) and (2), after "an officer of the Service" insert "or Welsh family proceedings officer".

11 In section 105(1) (interpretation), at the end insert-
   ""Welsh family proceedings officer" has the meaning given by section 35 of the Children Act 2004."

Criminal Justice and Court Services Act 2000 (c. 43)

12 The Criminal Justice and Court Services Act 2000 is amended as follows.

13 In section 12 (principal functions of CAFCASS), in subsection (1), after "the welfare of children" insert "other than children ordinarily resident in Wales".

14 In paragraph 1 of Schedule 2 (members of CAFCASS), for "ten" substitute "nine".

Adoption and Children Act 2002 (c. 38)

15 The Adoption and Children Act 2002 is amended as follows.

16 (1) Section 102 (officers of the Service) is amended as follows.

   (2) In subsection (1), at the end insert "or a Welsh family proceedings officer".

   (3) In subsection (7), after "officer of the Service" insert "or a Welsh family proceedings officer".

(4) After that subsection insert-
"(8) In this section and section 103 "Welsh family proceedings officer" has the meaning given by section 35 of the Children Act 2004."

17 In section 103 (rights of officers of the Service), in subsections (1) and (2), after "officer of the Service" insert "or a Welsh family proceedings officer".

Sexual Offences Act 2003 (c. 42)

18 In section 21 of the Sexual Offences Act 2003 (positions of trust), in subsection (12)(a), after "officer of the Service" insert "or Welsh family proceedings officer (within the meaning given by section 35 of the Children Act 2004)".

Schedule 4 Child minding and day care

See section 48.

1 Part 10A of the Children Act 1989 (c. 41) is amended as follows.	Makes amendments to the child-minding and day care provisions in Part 10A of the Children Act 1989.

Amendments relating to child minding and day care

Conditions imposed by justice of the peace or tribunal

2 (1) In section 79B(3)(d) and (4)(d), for "by the registration authority" substitute "under this Part". (2) In section 79G(2), omit "under section 79F(3)".	Makes conditions imposed by a court or the Care Standards Tribunal applicable to the registration authority (Ofsted in England and the Assembly in Wales) to enable enforcement action if conditions are breached.

Application fees

3   (1) In section 79E(2), at the end insert-
      "(c)   be accompanied by the prescribed fee."
 	
(2) In section 79F(1) and (2)-
    (a) after "on an application" insert "under section 79E";
    (b) omit paragraph (b) and the preceding "and".
	Makes minor adjustments to how fees are paid: fees are payable on application but the registration authority does not have to levy fees annually in future, that is fees could be paid monthly.

Fees payable by registered persons

4   (1) In section 79G(1), for "an annual fee" substitute "a fee".
 	
(2) In Schedule 9A-
    (a) in the heading before paragraph 7, omit "Annual";
    (b) in paragraph 7, for the words from "at prescribed times" to the end substitute
	Makes minor adjustments to how fees are paid: fees are payable on application but the registration authority does not have to levy fees annually in future, that is fees could be paid monthly.

", at or by the prescribed times, fees of the prescribed amounts in respect of the discharge by the registration authority of its functions under Part XA."

Waiver of disqualification

5   In Schedule 9A, in paragraph 4(3A)-
  (a) after "disqualified for registration" insert "(and may in particular provide for a person not to be disqualified for registration for the purposes of sub-paragraphs (4) and (5))";
  (b) in paragraph (b), omit "to his registration".

Clarifies the scope of disqualification waivers made by the registration authority.

Amendments relating to day care only

Qualification for registration

6   In section 79B(4)-
  (a) for paragraphs (a) and (b) substitute-
    "(a) he has made adequate arrangements to ensure that-
      (i) every person (other than himself and the responsible individual) looking after children on the premises is suitable to look after children under the age of eight; and
      (ii) every person (other than himself and the responsible individual) living or working on the premises is suitable to be in regular contact with children under the age of eight;
    (b) the responsible individual-
      (i) is suitable to look after children under the age of eight, or
      (ii) if he is not looking after such children, is suitable to be in regular contact with them;";

Enables the registration authority not to do a suitability check on all individuals employed by a provider to carry out childcare work but to assess whether the provider has procedures in place to do suitability checks.

(b) in subsection (5), for "(4)(b)" substitute "(4)(a)";
(c) after subsection (5) insert-
"(5ZA) For the purposes of subsection (4), "the responsible individual" means-
(a) in a case of one individual working on the premises in the provision of day care, that person;
(b) in a case of two or more individuals so working, the individual so working who is in charge."

Hotels etc

7   In Schedule 9A, after paragraph 2 insert-
"2A (1) Part XA does not apply to provision of day care in a hotel, guest house or other similar establishment for children staying in that establishment where-
(a) the provision takes place only between 6 pm and 2 am; and
(b) the person providing the care is doing so for no more than two different clients at the same time.
(2) For the purposes of sub-paragraph (1)(b), a "client" is a person at whose request (or persons at whose joint request) day care is provided for a child."

Provides a waiver for evening child minding services provided by hotels.

Prohibition in respect of disqualified persons

8   In Schedule 9A, in paragraph 4(4)-
(a) after "or be" insert "directly";
(b) omit ", or have any financial interest in,".

Removes the prohibition that a disqualified person cannot have a financial interest in the provision of childcare. Such a person can also have an interest in the management of the service provided it is not direct management.

plain guide to the Children Act 2004

Unincorporated associations

9　In Schedule 9A, after paragraph 5 insert-
"Provision of day care: unincorporated associations

5A　(1)　References in Part XA to a person, so far as relating to the provision of day care, include an unincorporated association.

(2)　Proceedings for an offence under Part XA which is alleged to have been committed by an unincorporated association must be brought in the name of the association (and not in that of any of its members).

(3)　For the purpose of any such proceedings, rules of court relating to the service of documents are to have effect as if the association were a body corporate.

(4)　In proceedings for an offence under Part XA brought against an unincorporated association, section 33 of the Criminal Justice Act 1925 and Schedule 3 to the Magistrates' Courts Act 1980 (procedure) apply as they do in relation to a body corporate.

(5)　A fine imposed on an unincorporated association on its conviction of an offence under Part XA is to be paid out of the funds of the association.

(6)　If an offence under Part XA committed by an unincorporated association is shown-
　(a)　to have been committed with the consent or connivance of an officer of the association or a member of its governing body, or
　(b)　to be attributable to any neglect on the part of such an officer or member, the officer or member as well as the association is guilty of the offence and liable to proceeded against and punished accordingly."

Allows an unincorporated association to register as a provider. Previously, members of an unincorporated association would have to register in their names individually.

Schedule 5 Repeals

See section 64.

Part 1 Plans

Short title and chapter	Extent of repeal
Children Act 1989 (c. 41)	In Schedule 2, paragraph 1A.
Education Act 1996 (c. 56)	Section 527A.
Education Act 1997 (c. 44)	Section 9.

School Standards and Framework Act 1998 (c. 31)	Section 2.
	Sections 6 and 7.
	Sections 26 to 26B.
	In section 27(2), the words "section 26,".
	Section 119(5)(b) and the preceding "and".
	Sections 120 and 121.
	In Schedule 6–
	    (a) paragraph 3(4)(b) and the preceding "and";
	    (b) paragraph 8(4).
	In Schedule 30, paragraph 144.

Learning and Skills Act 2000 (c. 21)	In Schedule 7–
	    (a) paragraph 35(2)(b);
	    (b) paragraph 42(2)(a).
	In Schedule 9, paragraphs 80 and 81.

Adoption and Children Act 2002 (c. 38)	Section 5.

Education Act 2002 (c. 32)	In section 150–
	    (a) subsections (2) to (4);
	    (b) in subsection (5), the words from "and early years development plans" to "childcare plans"".

These repeals come into force–
- (a) so far as relating to England, in accordance with provision made by order by the Secretary of State;
- (b) so far as relating to Wales, in accordance with provision so made by the Assembly.

Part 2 Child minding and day care

Short title and chapter	Extent of repeal
Children Act 1989 (c. 41)	In section 79F(1) and (2), paragraph (b) and the preceding "and". In section 79G(2), the words "under section 79F(3)". In Schedule 9A– (a) in paragraph 4(3A)(b), the words "to his registration"; (b) in paragraph 4(4), the words ", or have any financial interest in,"; (c) in the heading before paragraph 7, the word "Annual".

These repeals come into force–
- (a) so far as relating to England, in accordance with provision made by order by the Secretary of State;
- (b) so far as relating to Wales, in accordance with provision so made by the Assembly.

Part 3 Inspection of Local Education Authorities

Short title and chapter	Extent of repeal
Disability Discrimination Act 1995 (c. 50)	Section 28D(6).

This repeal comes into force–
- (a) so far as relating to England, in accordance with provision made by order by the Secretary of State;
- (b) so far as relating to Wales, in accordance with provision so made by the Assembly.

Part 4 Social services committees and departments

Short title and chapter	Extent of repeal
Children and Young Persons Act 1933 (c. 12)	In section 96(7), the words from "Subject to" to "that committee)".

Short title and chapter	Extent of repeal
Children and Young Persons Act 1963 (c. 37)	In section 56(2)– (a) the words "and subsection (1) of section 3 of the Local Authority Social Services Act 1970"; (b) the words "and section 2 of the said Act of 1970 respectively"
Local Authority Social Services Act 1970 (c. 42)	Sections 2 to 5.
Local Government Act 1972 (c. 70)	Section 101(9)(f).
Mental Health Act 1983 (c. 20)	In section 14, the words "of their social services department".
Police and Criminal Evidence Act 1984 (c. 60)	In section 63B(10), in the definition of "appropriate adult", the words "social services department".
Local Government and Housing Act 1989 (c. 42)	Section 13(2)(c). In Schedule 1, in paragraph 4(2)– (a) in paragraph (a) of the definition of "ordinary sub-committee", the words from "of the authority's" to "any other sub-committee"; and (b) the definition of "social services committee".
Criminal Justice Act 1991 (c. 53)	In sections 43(5) and 65(1)(b) and (1B)(a), the words "social services department".
Crime (Sentences) Act 1997 (c. 43)	In section 31(2A)(b), the words "social services department of the". In Schedule 1, in the table in paragraph 9(6), the words "social services department".
Crime and Disorder Act 1998 (c. 37)	The words "social services department" in– (a) section 1AA(9) and (10)(a); (b) section 8(8)(b); (c) section 9(2B)(b); (d) section 11(8)(a); (e) section 18(4)(a); (f) section 39(5)(b); (g) section 65(7)(b); (h) section 98(3) (in the words substituted by that provision).
Powers of Criminal Courts (Sentencing) Act 2000 (c. 6)	The words "social services department" in– (a) section 46(5)(a) and (b); (b) section 69(4)(b), (6)(a) and (10)(a); (c) section 73(5); (d) section 74(5)(b) and (7)(a); (e) section 103(3)(b) and (5)(a); (f) section 162(2)(a) and (b).
Local Government Act 2000 (c. 22)	Section 102(1).

Short title and chapter	Extent of repeal
Criminal Justice and Court Services Act 2000 (c. 43) Criminal Justice Act 2003 (c. 44)	In section 64(6), in the definition of "appropriate adult", the words "social services department". The words "social services department" in– (a) section 158(2)(b); (b) section 161(8)(b); (c) section 199(4)(b); (d) paragraph 5(4) of Schedule 38 (in the words substituted by that provision).

These repeals come into force–
- (a) so far as relating to England, in accordance with provision made by order by the Secretary of State;
- (b) so far as relating to Wales, in accordance with provision so made by the Assembly.

Part 5 Reasonable punishment

Short title and chapter	Extent of repeal
Children and Young Persons Act 1933 (c. 12)	Section 1(7).

This repeal comes into force at the same time as section 56.

Part 6 Child safety orders

Short title and chapter	Extent of repeal
Crime and Disorder Act 1998 (c. 37)	Section 12(6)(a) and (7).

These repeals come into force at the same time as section 58.

References

DEPARTMENT FOR EDUCATION AND SKILLS (2004a). *Draft Statutory Guidance on the Role and Responsibilities of the Director of Children's Services and the Lead Member for Children's Services* [online]. Available: http://www.dfes.gov.uk/consultations/conDetails.cfm?consultationId=1276 [2 December, 2004].

DEPARTMENT FOR EDUCATION AND SKILLS (2004b). *Every Child Matters: Change for Children. Working with Voluntary and Community Organisations to Deliver Change for Children and Young People* [online]. Available: http://www.everychildmatters.gov.uk/_content/documents/DfES-ECM-Work%20Vol+Comm.pdf [2 December, 2004].

DEPARTMENT FOR EDUCATION AND SKILLS (2004c). *Every Child Matters: Next Steps* [online]. Available: http://www.everychildmatters.gov.uk/_content/documents/EveryChildMattersNextSteps.pdf [2 December, 2004].

DEPARTMENT FOR EDUCATION AND SKILLS (2004d). *Information Sharing Databases in Children's Services: Consultation on Recording Practitioner Details for Potentially Sensitive Services and Recording Concern About a Child or Young Person* [online]. Available: http://www.dfes.gov.uk/consultations/conDetails.cfm?consultationId=1280 [2 December, 2004].

DEPARTMENT FOR EDUCATION AND SKILLS (2004e). *Safeguarding Children in Education* (DfES/0027/2004) [online]. Available: http://publications.teachernet.gov.uk/eOrderingDownload/DfES-0027-2004.pdf [2 December, 2004].

DEPARTMENT FOR EDUCATION AND SKILLS, DEPARTMENT OF HEALTH and HOME OFFICE (2003). *Keeping Children Safe: The Government's Response to the Victoria Climbie Inquiry Report and Joint Chief Inspector's Report Safeguarding Children* (Cm. 5861). London: The Stationery Office.

DEPARTMENT OF HEALTH (2004). *National Service Framework for Children, Young People and Maternity Services: Core Standards* [online]. Available: http://www.dh.gov.uk/assetRoot/04/09/05/66/04090566.pdf [2 December, 2004]

DEPARTMENT OF HEALTH, HOME OFFICE and DEPARTMENT FOR EDUCATION AND EMPLOYMENT (1999). *Working Together to Safeguard Children*. London: The Stationery Office.

HM TREASURY (2003). *Every Child Matters* (Cm. 5860) [online]. Available: http://www.everychildmatters.gov.uk/_content/documents/EveryChildMatters.pdf [2 December, 2004].

OFFICE FOR STANDARDS IN EDUCATION (2004). *Every Child Matters: Inspecting Services for Children and Young People. A Discussion Paper* [online]. Available: http://www.ofsted.gov.uk/publications/index.cfm?fuseaction=pubs.displayfile&id=3637&type=pdf [2 December, 2004].

OFFICE OF THE HIGH COMMISSIONER FOR HUMAN RIGHTS (2004). *Convention on the Rights of the Child* [online]. Available: http://www.unhchr.ch/html/menu3/b/k2crc.htm [2 December, 2004].

UNITED KINGDOM. PARLIAMENT. HOUSE OF COMMONS (2003). *The Victoria Climbie Enquiry* (Cm. 5730). http://www.victoria-climbie-inquiry.org.uk/finreport/report.pdf [2 December, 2004].

UNITED KINGDOM. PARLIAMENT. HOUSE OF COMMONS (2004). *Choosing Health: Making Healthy Choices Easier* (Cm. 6374) [online]. Available: http://www.dh.gov.uk/PublicationsAndStatistics/Publications/PublicationsPolicyAndGuidance/PublicationsPolicyAndGuidanceArticle/fs/en?CONTENT_ID=4094550&chk=aN5Cor [2 December, 2004].

THE VICTORIA CLIMBIE INQUIRY (2003). 'Victoria Climbie Report calls for radical change in the management of public services for children and families', *The Victoria Climbie Inquiry*, 28 January [online]. Available: http://www.victoria-climbie-inquiry.org.uk/News_Update/news_update.htm [7 December, 2004].

WELSH ASSEMBLY GOVERNMENT (2000). *Children and Young People: a Framework for Partnership* [online]. Available: http://www.wales.gov.uk/subichildren/content/consultations/young/q262a360%20english.pdf [7 December, 2004].

WELSH ASSEMBLY GOVERNMENT (2004). *Children and Young People: Rights to Action* [online]. Available: http://www.wales.gov.uk/subichildren/content/consultations/cyp04-cover-e.pdf [7 December, 2004].

Further reading

BICHARD, M. (2004). *The Bichard Inquiry Report* (HC 653) [online]. Available: http://www.bichardinquiry.org.uk/10663/html/titlepage_copyright.htm [2 December, 2004].

DEPARTMENT FOR EDUCATION AND SKILLS (2004). *Commissioning Alternative Provision. Consultation* [online]. Available: http://www.dfes.gov.uk/consultations/downloadableDocs/ACF65D.pdf [2 December, 2004].

DEPARTMENT FOR EDUCATION AND SKILLS (2004). *Commissioning Checklist: a Step-by-Step Guide to Better Planning and Commissioning of Placements and Services for Looked After Children and Children with Special Educational Needs and Disabilities in Residential Schools* [online]. Available: http://www.dfes.gov.uk/choiceprotects/pdfs/Commissioningchecklist.pdf [2 December, 2004].

DEPARTMENT FOR EDUCATION AND SKILLS (2004). *Department for Education and Skills: Five Year Strategy for Children and Learners* (Cm. 6272) [online]. Available: http://www.dfes.gov.uk/publications/5yearstrategy/docs/DfES5Yearstrategy1.rtf [2 December, 2004].

DEPARTMENT FOR EDUCATION AND SKILLS (2004). *Identifying and Maintaining Contact with Children Missing or at Risk of Going Missing from Education: Process Steps. Good Practice Guide* [online]. Available: http://www.dfes.gov.uk/educationprotects/upload/ACF4F6.doc [2 December, 2004].

DEPARTMENT FOR EDUCATION AND SKILLS (2004). *Removing Barriers to Achievement: the Government's Strategy for SEN* [online]. Available: http://www.teachernet.gov.uk/wholeschool/sen/senstrategy [24 August, 2004].

DEPARTMENT FOR EDUCATION AND SKILLS (2004, forthcoming). *Every Child Matters: Change for Children in the Criminal Justice System*. London: DfES.

DEPARTMENT FOR EDUCATION AND SKILLS (2004, forthcoming). *Every Child Matters: Change for Children in Health Services*. London: DfES.

DEPARTMENT FOR EDUCATION AND SKILLS (2004, forthcoming). *Every Child Matters: Change for Children in Schools*. London: DfES.

DEPARTMENT FOR EDUCATION AND SKILLS (2004, forthcoming). *Every Child Matters: Change for Children in Social Care*. London: DfES.

DEPARTMENT OF HEALTH (2003). *What to Do If You're Worried a Child is Being Abused: Full Report. Children's Services Guidance*. London: The Stationery Office.

DEPARTMENT OF HEALTH (2004). *The Chief Nursing Officer's Review of the Nursing, Midwifery and Health Visiting Contribution to Vulnerable Young Children and Young People* [online]. Available: http://www.dh.gov.uk/assetRoot/04/08/72/21/04087221.pdf [2 December, 2004].

DEPARTMENT OF HEALTH (2004). *National Standards, Local Action: Health and Social Care Standards and Planning Framework 2005/06–2007/08* [online]. Available: http://www.dh.gov.uk/assetRoot/04/08/60/58/04086058.pdf [2 December, 2004].

DEPARTMENT OF HEALTH (2004). *NHS Direct Commissioning Framework April 2004-05. Guidance for Primary Care Trusts on Commissioning NHS Direct Services from 1 April 2004* [online]. Available: http://www.nhsdirect.nhs.uk/misc/fGatewayfeb04.pdf [2 December, 2004].

HM TREASURY (2003). *Every Child Matters: Change for Children* (Cm. 5860) [online]. Available: http://www.everychildmatters.gov.uk/_content/documents/EveryChildMatters.pdf [2 December, 2004].

HM TREASURY (2004). *Child Poverty Review* [online]. Available: http://www.hm-treasury.gov.uk/media/985/CC/childpoverty_complete_290704.pdf [2 December, 2004].

HOME OFFICE (2003). *Youth Justice: the Next Steps. Companion Document to 'Every Child Matters'* [online]. Available: http://www.everychildmatters.gov.uk/_content/documents/youth-justice-english.pdf [2 December, 2004].

HOME OFFICE (2004). *Confident Communities in a Secure Britain: the Home Office Strategic Plan 2004–08* (Cm. 6287) [online]. Available: http://www.homeoffice.gov.uk/docs3/strategicplan.pdf [2 December, 2004].

HOME OFFICE DRUGS STRATEGY DIRECTORATE (2002). *Updated Drug Strategy 2002* [online]. Available: http://www.drugs.gov.uk/ReportsandPublications/NationalStrategy/1038840683/Updated_Drug_Strategy_2002.pdf [2 December, 2004].

OFFICE OF THE DEPUTY PRIME MINISTER (2003). *National Procurement Strategy for Local Government* [online]. Available: http://www.odpm.gov.uk/stellent/groups/odpm_localgov/documents/page/odpm_locgov_029231-01.hcsp#P20_469 [2 December, 2004].

OFFICE OF THE DEPUTY PRIME MINISTER (2004). *The Future of Local Government: Developing a 10 Year Vision* [online]. Available: http://www.odpm.gov.uk/stellent/groups/odpm_localgov/documents/downloadable/odpm_locgov_030563.pdf [2 December, 2004].

SOCIAL EXCLUSION UNIT (2003). *A Better Education for Children in Care* [online]. Available: http://www.socialexclusionunit.gov.uk/downloaddoc.asp?id=32 [2 December, 2004].

UNITED KINGDOM. PARLIAMENT. HOUSE OF COMMONS (2004). *Opportunity for All: Sixth Annual Report 2004* (Cm. 6239) [online]. Available: http://www.dwp.gov.uk/ofa/reports/2004/pdf/report_04.pdf. [2 December, 2004].

UNITED KINGDOM. PARLIAMENT. HOUSE OF COMMONS (2004). *Parental Separation: Children's Needs and Parents' Responsibilities* (Cm 6273) [online]. Available: http://www.dfes.gov.uk/childrensneeds/docs/DfesChildrensNeeds.pdf [2 December, 2004].

UNIVERSITY OF EAST ANGLIA and NATIONAL CHILDREN'S BUREAU (2004). *National Evaluation of Children's Trusts: Phase 1 Interim Report* [online]. Available: http://www.everychildmatters.gov.uk/_content/documents/Evaluation%20of%20childrens%20trusts%20preliminary%20report%202004.pdf [2 December, 2004].

WORKING GROUP ON 14-19 REFORM (2004). *14-19 Curriculum and Qualifications Reform: Final Report of the Working Group on 14-19 Reform.* London: DfES.

List of Acts

These Acts can be accessed from The United Kingdom Parliament website at http://www.legislation.hmso.gov.uk/acts.htm

Adoption and Children Act 2002

Care Standards Act 2000

Children Act 1989

Children Act 2004

Crime and Disorder Act 1998

Criminal Justice Act 2003

Criminal Justice and Court Services Act 2000

Criminal Justice and Public Order Act 1994

Data Protection Act 1998

Education Act 1997

Education Act 2002

Health and Social Care (Community Health and Standards) Act 2003

Learning and Skills Act 2000

Local Authority Social Services Act 1970

Matrimonial and Family Proceedings Act 1984

Protection of Children Act 1999

Tax Credits Act 2002

List of acronyms

ACEO	Association of Chief Education Officers (now known as Association of Directors of Education and Children's Services)
ACPC	Area Child Protection Committee
ADECS	Association of Directors of Education and Children's Services
ADSS	Association of Directors of Social Services
ALI	Adult Learning Inspectorate
CAFCASS	Children and Family Court Advisory and Support Service
ConfEd	The Confederation of Education and Children's Services Managers
CSA	Children's Services Authority
CYPP	Children and Young People's Plan
DCS	Director of Children's Services
Dfes	Department for Education and Skills
DoH	Department of Health
DWP	Department of Work and Pensions
ELWa	Education and Learning Wales
Estyn	Her Majesty's Inspectorate for Education and Training in Wales
HMCI	Her Majesty's Chief Inspector of Schools
IAG	Inter-Agency Group
JAR	Joint Area Review
LA	Local Authority
LEA	Local Education Authority
LGA	Local Government Association
LSC	Learning and Skills Council
LSCB	Local Safeguarding Children Board
NAfW	National Assembly for Wales
NCB	National Children's Bureau
NCH	National Children's Homes
NCSL	National College for School Leadership
NCVCCO	National Council for Voluntary Childcare Organisations
NSF	National Service Framework

NSPCC	National Society for the Prevention of Cruelty to Children Education and Children's Services
Ofsted	Office for Standards in Education
PCT	Primary Care Trust
SHA	Strategic Health Authority
SOLACE	Society of Local Authority Chief Executives
UNCRC	United Nations Convention on the Rights of the Child
WFPO	Welsh Family Proceedings Officer